Joanne Seabloom
+
Claire Carr

HENRY FOREVER:
THE GIFT OF LIFE

HENRY FORVER:
The Gift of Life

by

Claire Carr and Joanne Seabloom

Photographs by Ken Seabloom

Wynship Arts
Maryville, Tennessee

Contents

ODE TO THE NEWFOUNDLAND

"They're too big."
"They shed too much."
"They drool too much."
Their size is small
In comparison to the amount of love they share.
No matter how much hair they shed,
There is always plenty left in which to bury your face.
And the drool . . .well, always have that towel handy!
Don't they know, though, that it gets no better than this?
Those eyes . . . their hearts . . .so big and ever giving you love.
Their faces speak to you of kindness, of joie de vivre,
Of a knowledge that they have it all figured out.
Life is for love and laughter,
For being there to comfort and caress.
They'll shed a tear for you, never for themselves.
They protect and wrap themselves around you,
And enter the very core of your being.
They make you smile,
When you thought you had nothing left to smile about.
They fill you with a love that knows no boundaries.
You might not always know what they want,
But they always know what you need.
They are to be treasured as they are treasures.
They are Newfoundlands.

(With permission of the author, Naomi Gofberg)

DEDICATION

In memory of a very special Newfoundland, Henry 1st, this story has been written to honour each individual who has given new life and spirit to a dog, which, for whatever reason, needed a new home.

❤

ACKNOWLEDGMENTS

A very genuine thank you to Ann Thibault, a member of the Newf-List, and Claire's long time friend and former business partner. She mailed a copy of Joanne's story about Henry when it first appeared on the Newf-List, suggesting, "Claire, you might be interested in this." Because of that letter, HENRY FOREVER: The Gift of Life, has become a reality.

The authors wish to sincerely thank our husbands, John Carr and Ken Seabloom. They have given us the freedom and encouragement to enjoy this project, as well as many other adventures with our animals too numerous to mention.

We include here a special tribute to Ken from Joanne for always being there when she needed him.

Ken provided the photographs for our book, as he did for the Newf-List and the Ginnie virtual postcard.

Joanne thanks her parents, Geraldine and Gordon Welburn, for their never ending love and encouragement. Geraldine's beautiful drawing of Henry was included without her permission. Joanne and Claire wanted to surprise her!

A special thank you to Brock and Dirk Seabloom, who were always ready to lend Joanne a helping hand with Henry or any of her four-footed family when extra care was needed.

There are innumerable people from the Newf-list that provided support and encouragement during the last months of Henry's life. They helped to keep up Joanne's spirits with their notes of kindness.

We extend our appreciation to Dr. Dennis Fetko, AKA Dr. Dog, who kindly gave us a knowledgeable point of view to help understand young Henry's behavior.

Ann Elliott, of Fall Creek, Wisconsin, has lived with Newfoundlands for fifty years. Ann introduced Claire to Newfs long before they became sisters-in-law. She has devoted much time as editor and advisor on this manuscript. Thank you Ann!

We thank Ula Miller of Sun City, Arizona for her professional attention to detail as she worked through the pages of Henry's story.

Marjorie Gilbert was inspired by Henry's life and shares her love and understanding of Newfoundlands as poetry. We thank her for permission to reprint her poems.

Ruth Landmann sent Joanne a collection of poetry about humans and our connection with our dogs. Some will appear in this book. Thank you Ruth.

Henry's date of birth is stated as December 6, 1980. There is no longer any paper work available to verify this. He did live a long and fascinating life and we are happy to share it with you.

Part One is presented in story form. The stories are true. With the exception of the Seabloom family, all names are fictitious.

Part Two and Part Four are actual e-mail communications. Special thanks to those of you who granted us permission to use your names.

You represent twelve countries on four continents. You have helped to make Henry's story unique. Thank you also for your enthusiasm about our project.

Claire Carr and Joanne Seabloom

Claire Carr   *Joanne Seabloom*

WHAT THE BEHAVIORIST SAYS

Henry bounced from one foster family to another. He simply would not stay in any foster home for long . . . unless he was chained.

Question: What creates this behavior in a dog?

Dr. Dennis Fetko, Ph.D., of San Diego, California, is a full-time trainer and behaviorist with over thirty years of international experience with several species and a nationally syndicated radio talk show host: "Dr. Dog Talks Animals."
Dr. Fetko responded to our question.

"A dog learns by everything you do with and near it. The only requirement for learning is perception. If the dog perceives you, it's learning something. It may be learning to take you seriously, to ignore you or fear you, or that being with you is great fun. You teach it either what you want it to know or what you don't want it to know. But, since it learns by everything it perceives, you cannot teach nothing.

Henry literally learned that despite being the best dog he knew how to be, no home, pack or territory wanted him permanently. Dogs in this circumstance often leave on their own for their own reasons instead of waiting for this home and family to throw them out like all the others did.

Behaviorists treat a condition called Show Dog Syndrome. I've been retained to work with dogs that were born into one home/family, sold to another, traveled with another, were trained and campaigned by another, boarded with another, bred in another, all before they are three years old! They commonly act nicely towards all, and strongly, permanently bond with none. They never learned HOW to bond.

But not only won't some show people openly admit this, they'll typically strongly deny it. Even if they truly care about such bonds and the quality of the dog's life, privately they complain about it and curse it.

If they don't truly care about the dog or the bond, well, that's how this got started in the first place. When status and ego, dog titles and ribbons, and dollars are more important to an owner than the quality of the dog's life, is any of this a surprise?

And then an owner wonders why the dog doesn't bond with and behave toward them and their families like a pet owner's companion does.

Thank all the gods Henry found and formed a permanent, quality home."

❤

Until one has loved an animal, a part of one's soul remains unawakened.

-Anatole France-

❤

PART ONE

CHAPTER ONE

Imprinted by Newfoundlands

It was early in 1997 that Joanne Seabloom entered the lives of people around the world via the Internet with those wonderful stories about Henry, her sixteen-year-old Newfoundland. She had only a mild interest in computers. They were something her husband used in his business. Then one day, motivated by her love of the breed, she started surfing the Internet. She found a site for Newfoundland Dogs. The web page asked her name and requested a bit of information about her dogs. Innocently, she shared one account after another of her adventures living with this strong willed and determined dog. With a click of the send button on her computer the messages went to a Newfoundland dog lovers' site called the Newf-List.

It didn't take long for her to realize that Henry had quite a following. Why? According to the most recent statistics of The Health and Longevity Committee of the Newfoundland Club of America the average life span of the Newfoundland dog is 9.4 years. When Joanne joined the Newf-List Henry was sixteen. Why had Henry lived so long? Combinations of factors came into play: basic good health, a powerful determined personality and one woman's knowledgeable and loving care.

The story began in 1970, when their parents told fifteen year old Joanne and her twelve-year-old sister, Sandra, that they were going to sell their home in North Vancouver, British Columbia. The girls were invited to help as they searched for a boat to be their new home. They were assured it would be just right for

3

all of them. The deal included their cat and dog.

Wispy was Joanne's mixed-breed puppy that looked like a Bearded Collie. She became a part of the family when Joanne bought her for fifteen dollars from a family who laughingly fed the pup marijuana. Wispy was always sickly and plagued with chronic ear infections. Joanne remembers the feel of the ailing dog's coat against her arms as she carried Wispy on one of her frequent visits to the veterinarian. She walked because she wasn't allowed to ride on a bus with the dog.

In anticipation of life on board a boat, Joanne remembers urging, "Don't worry about Wispy, I'll take care of her and clean up after her."

The family considered many possibilities, sometimes going for a sail on a boat they liked. One day, south of Vancouver, they found just the right boat, the Sereph II. Joanne describes the sloop as a thirty six-foot double-ender of Hilliard design. It was a beautiful wooden boat that was made in England. Using the language of a seafarer, she comfortably recalls memories of the home where she lived for two years.

> "It had our complete galley kitchen, furnace, and a table that could be lowered to make a comfortable spare double bed with the seat cushions. There were steps to the wheelhouse with a beautiful brass compass and the mahogany steering wheel. There were seats where we sat as we sailed the boat. There were brass oil lamps throughout the boat. One of my jobs was to keep the brass polished and gleaming. Behind the cockpit, we stepped down into the aft cabin that was my parent's bedroom. There was a comfy

double bunk and cupboards. The TV sat on a shelf opposite on the starboard side. We could move it to the main cabin as well. Then came the main head. There was even a bathtub. Then there was another storage locker. On deck was the mast. It was solid wood. Even back then it was getting to be unusual with many people favouring the modern lightweight aluminum. There was a self-steering vane at the stern. The ropes (called sheets) attached to the sails and the docking lines were always kept coiled neatly and there was always the smell of fresh varnish. Everything was AC/DC power."

It was actually closer to the vet's office after they moved onto the Sereph II. When she was sixteen, Joanne took a part time job at an aquarium shop to help pay Wispy's vet bills. Even with loving care, Wispy didn't live to be a year old.

Joanne's parents moved the Sereph II to Mosquito Creek Marina in North Vancouver. As the young girl from British Columbia stepped down the yellow cedar planks of her floating home, she stepped into an experience that would change her life forever.

Beside the ramp was an old log salvage boat named Golden Hair. A man named John lived on board with his ancient canine, Bear. The teenager loved the old dog from the very beginning. Every time she passed by she stopped to give Bear a pat and a treat.

"The dog smelled really bad, like old seawater," Joanne remembers. "Although she was a black dog, her thick coat was now red gold and nearly one solid mat. John loved his dog very much and proudly told me that Bear was a purebred Newfoundland, born to be a water dog. He didn't think he would ever own another one because the coat was very hard to take care of. He said he had her shaved once a year."

Occasionally the young girl had to rescue Bear from drowning because she no longer could swim. Her matted coat soaked up water and she couldn't stay afloat.

When Joanne was sixteen she completed a course at a dog grooming school. John wanted her to shave Bear. She tried. But the clippers wouldn't cut through Bear's coat. Each day, using scissors, she would cut away some of the mats.

However, before her task was complete, she walked down the ramp one morning to find Golden Hair gone from her slip. There was a can of stew left on the dock weighting down a five-dollar bill. And there was Bear! She was lying under the ramp. The old dog seemed unusually lethargic. Instead of grooming and cutting away mats, the sixteen-year old sat beside Bear and patted and comforted her. That same day as Joanne sat holding the old Newfoundland in her arms, Bear passed away.

The cost to have an animal picked up by the SPCA was exactly five dollars. Joanne believes John must have known the end was near and couldn't face losing Bear. He also knew Joanne would care for her as long as the old dog lived.

Joanne became Mrs. Kenneth Seabloom in February of 1980, and began a life that would include many pets. She had her Arabian gelding, Phaedran, and a rare Vinaceous Amazon parrot named Sailor. She said that she and her crew "came as a trio." Soon after their marriage Ken had a horse of his own.

That same year, on Galiano Island, not far from North Vancouver, a litter of thirteen Newfoundlands was born. They all lived. One of those pups was sold to a young couple on the island. They named him Henry 1st.

In 1982, Ken and Joanne welcomed their first-born son, Dirk, and the family moved to a one-acre hobby farm in Mission, BC. Their little home was surrounded by blackberry bushes, honeysuckle and flowering quince. A pasture on one side of the house had a pond that teemed with fish and turtles. There was room for their growing menagerie. Phaedran and the parrot were soon joined by four types of show rabbits, French and English Angoras, Netherland Dwarfs and Mini Lops. A neighbour gave them an old Shetland pony, Buddy Boy, because their children had outgrown him. Then came a Miniature horse mare, Sassy. Her foals, Sunshine and Cameo are still a part of the Seabloom clan.

Ken went to town one day to pick up hay and came home with a little extra, a Husky-mix puppy. They named her Kobe. She was not the Newfoundland or St. Bernard they hoped to have but they enjoyed her. She suffered severe hip dysplasia and had to be put to sleep at a young age.

The year was 1983. One day, a friend of Joanne's called to say that there was a Newfoundland advertised in the paper, "Free to a good home." Ken and Joanne went to see her and brought her home. Her name was Rascal. She had spent her three years living in a six-foot pen. She adored children and needed attention. She was a dream come true for the Seablooms. She got along well with Kobe and was gentle with their young son, Dirk.

Rascal was a high energy, happy dog. She was great in the house, but if she went out on lead she was uncontrollable. She loved to run! Her favorite sport was dashing up behind you and trying to run between your legs! Frequently she knocked Joanne down. This was not good since Joanne was expecting their second child.

Shortly after Brock was born in 1984, Joanne had an accident on her horse resulting in knee surgery. She was resting on the chesterfield with brand new baby Brock on top of her. Ken had gone to a job interview and Rascal proved her natural babysitting skills. Dirk was playing on the living room floor. The Newfoundland lay across the doorway keeping the two-year-old in the room. She spent the day standing up every time he tried to climb over her then lying down to block Dirk if he tried to crawl through the doorway.

Their neighbors had a duck pond. One morning Rascal jumped the fence and headed for the water. She thought it was fun to pounce on ducklings and watch them bob to the surface somewhere else. Joanne jumped the fence too. She grabbed Rascal by the tail and desperately tried to reach her collar. She was standing waist deep in water trying to protect the ducklings when the neighbor charged out of his house yelling, "If that dog ever comes over here again, I'll shoot it!"

Even though they loved Rascal dearly they feared for her safety. They were fortunate to find another home for her, where she had a Newfoundland for company. It was about an hour's drive away. Many times after the adoption they drove by. It was comforting to see that she was a happy dog.

A month later, the neighbor asked where the big dog was. When he learned what they had done he said, "I really wouldn't have shot your dog!"

Rascal is remembered as a wonderful Newfoundland. Both Ken and Joanne believe she is the reason they were so determined to find another to be a part of their growing family.

Puppies were too expensive for the young family to afford. They always checked the ads in the local paper, but it was a frustrating and endless search. Joanne volunteered for the local humane society hoping that one would come available. She never gave up her dream that they would find another Newfoundland that needed a home.

Henry's life was changing too. Because of a divorce his lifestyle changed. He started to wander. The long search for the family he could love was underway. Henry was four years old.

CHAPTER TWO

Duchess: Preamble to Henry

The year was 1987. In the last two years Henry had firmly established his reputation as a wanderer. He never found a place where he was content to call home. He kept searching.

"I really want a Newfoundland to raise with our boys, Ken, but we just can't afford a puppy."

Joanne looked at her husband, pleading for sympathy, advice, direction. "I've talked to all the breeders I can find, and it is always the same. A puppy still costs too much money."

He looked at her and smiled. "Keep looking for that second-hand Newf."

"You know the answer to that one! We have had our names in for a rescue Newf ever since we moved to Mission. Every local rescue club I talked with said Newfs are rarely available. And, if one turns up, their friends always get first dibs!" Her voice expressed her exasperation.

"It just isn't fair," she sighed.

"Okay, okay, now just take it easy," Ken soothed. "Getting all upset about stuff you can't control isn't going to help." Ken was thoughtful for a moment then suggested, "Why don't you stop volunteering for the SPCA? We will never be able to get what we want if we keep taking those homeless dogs. It is costing us a fortune to feed, de-worm and care for those unwanted animals."

Joanne frowned at him. "Alright, I'll think about it," she sighed. "I figured we'd have a better chance of getting one before it goes to a rescue group. It's been nearly three years! And, I am really sick of taking in homeless dogs and cats. There is no end to it. And, there is never a Newf."

She was quiet, obviously processing an idea. Ken knew the signals.

Joanne took a deep breath and looked at her husband. "Okay! I'll do this. I'll make some posters and we'll put them up around town. You can take some when you go out. We will put them every where we go. Maybe, someone will . . . well, let's just hope!"

She headed for the desk drawer where paper and markers were stored, gathered up the necessary materials and made space on the table. "While Brock is asleep, I have time to do a few," she said, as much to herself as to her husband.

Ken smiled. For the moment he had things under control.

"We're pretty broke, but you can call the local paper," he suggested. "It is early enough that maybe they can get it into tomorrow's edition." And, as an after thought, "we can put an ad in the Buy and Sell paper, it goes all over the place and it is free."

"Mmm," Joanne murmured, so dedicated to her project that she was hardly aware that she responded to his offer.

Soon there were ads in papers of nearby towns. Notices appeared on every available bulletin board.

A few days passed. The phone rang and Joanne answered.

"Hello. Are you, ah . . .are you still looking for a Newfoundland dog?" A young woman's voice inquired.

"Yes! Oh, yes!" Joanne answered, almost breathless with disbelief and excitement.

"I work as a waitress in a pub in a neighboring town. I saw your ad when I was in the laundromat. One of our patrons has a Newfoundland dog, I think."

The reality of the woman's words slowly filled Joanne with a strange numbness. She felt like she was in a dream. She heard herself saying, "Is this dog looking for a home?"

"It might be. The dog never stays home. It hangs around the store all the time." The waitress spoke hurriedly. "It is big and hairy. I'm pretty sure it's a Newfoundland dog. I will speak to the owner for you. Thanks, gotta go." And she was gone.

"Wait!" Joanne called out. But the voice was gone. With the telephone tone ringing in her ear, she realized she had no information; no name, no identification, no facts to work with, just a voice to remember. A voice that said somewhere out there, there might be a Newfoundland. She was stunned. Slowly she reached to hang up the phone.

Two nights later a man called. "Hello," he said. "Sally from the pub said she talked to you about my Newfoundland dog." His voice was raspy and coarse. He cleared his throat and continued. "I'd be willing to sell her. She's not happy here, never stays home. If you think you'd like to take a look at her, she is always hangin' around the Lake Eroche store."

Joanne listened carefully. "Yes sir, we would like . . ."

"Okay, then." And the man hung up.

"What was that all about?" Ken asked, as he looked up from the book in his lap.

She made eye contact with her husband but said nothing. "Joanne?"

"Remember when the waitress from the pub called about that Newfoundland dog?"

"Yes! Was she calling back?" Ken looked surprised.

"No," she said slowly, teasing a little. "It was the owner saying he'd sell us his dog!" Then, almost an afterthought, "It's a female."

It was already dark and a Friday night. The kids were in bed. "Can we go in the morning?" she asked. "Early?" Her knees were weak and she sank back down into her chair.

"You bet we can!" Ken said, "You bet we can."

Ken put his book on the table and moved toward Joanne's chair. He stood over her smiling. "Joanne, what would you think of . . .of going out there tonight? It isn't that far. We will have to take the boys. We ought to be able to go, see the dog and be back in a couple of hours."

"And if we don't go tonight something could happen to her," Joanne said as she made a dash for the boys' room.

She turned to her husband, smiling. "Can you believe this? Maybe, just maybe we have a new dog! I'll go wake the boys and get them ready, Ken. It'll just take a couple of minutes."

The truck sped through the darkness. Getting there would be easy. Someone in town could give them directions to the store.

There was laughter, then silence as the boys' parents pro- cessed private thoughts, then both talked at the same time. After so long it was hard to imagine there was really going to be a Newf in their lives. Maybe they had found a companion for their sons, a dream come true.

"You know, Ken," Joanne admitted after a long silence, "If this dog has hip dysplasia, I don't think I want to buy her."

He understood. In the next few moments he relived the anguish and heartbreak they both felt when they lost Kobe. "I agree," was his simple reply.

"There's the store!" Joanne pointed ahead and off to the left. A soft light shown from inside. There was a small light on the porch, just enough to see the two steps that led to the door. The truck slowed and Ken made his way into the end of a row of parked cars and stopped.

In the darkness they could barely make out a large black shape lying in the parking lot. Joanne opened the truck door and suddenly there was a large face pressed gently against her lap. "Ken," she whispered, "it's almost as if she has been waiting for us!"

Joanne turned to remind the boys to stay inside the truck. She smiled, they were snuggled in blankets sound asleep.

Ken took out his flashlight and they both got out to greet the big dog. She was openly friendly. The light focused on her black body. "She is a skeleton!" he said. "Even through all that coat, she is skin and bones! Joanne, she's limping. It looks like a bad hip."

Through the darkness their eyes met. Their thoughts were on the same track.

Ken didn't hesitate. "Back in a minute," he said as he hurried into the store to find out where the owner lived and get directions.

Joanne ran her hands over the dog's big frame. Lots of coat . . . tall. . . with a wagging tail she could feel in the darkness. So friendly! "Why are you so thin?" she wondered. Watching her favor the bad leg, she knew in her heart she would like to have this dog anyway.

"Okay, let's go," said Ken, keys in hand. "It's not very far, straight up this road. I told them we were taking the dog with us and go talk with the owner. They seemed eager to have her gone." He lifted the bony frame into the back of the truck, "In you go girl," he said. The canopy door clicked shut, and they pulled out of the driveway into the darkness.

"Did you see Sally?" Joanne asked.

"No, but I asked. She's off Friday, Saturday and Sunday."

They traveled the distance to the owners home in silence.

The elderly gentleman that welcomed the Seablooms showed some surprise that they brought the dog with them. It was obvious the man was nearly blind. His small duplex gave some indications that he did try to care for the dog. There were two armchairs in his living room, one for him, the other for her. There was a forty-pound bag of dog food with the top rolled down sitting by the front door and a bucket of water near by.

"What's her name," Joanne queried, opening the door to many questions she had for him.

He said he couldn't remember. "Maybe Princess, or somethin' like that." He admitted he just called her Dog. He was very vague about her past. She did come from a breeder who wasn't interested in her anymore since she was no longer producing puppies. He said he took her because he was very fond of her. All he ever said about her origin was "she came from upcountry." She did have one pup after he got her. He gave the pup to a farmer.

Did he really mean he "took her"? she asked herself. He was old, maybe forgetful, but there was something else going on here. She listened and kept her thoughts to herself.

Despite her general condition and a terribly atrophied left hind leg, the Seablooms bought her for forty dollars and took her home.

The next day was Saturday. The veterinarian would not be in until Monday morning.

They spent the weekend pampering their new family member. The boys were thrilled. Although she was weak, she showed genuine happiness and welcomed their attentions. Grooming, and trying to decide on a new name were the order of the day. They tried Princess and other names that she might know. Finally Joanne said, "Duchess." Her head came up. She looked alert. Right then, Dog became Duchess.

Joanne cooked oatmeal and mixed it with meat and gravy. She served frequent small tasty meals during the weekend to help her put on some weight. She called on her medical knowledge and her own resources. She knew how to care for ailing animals.

Early Monday morning the Seablooms arrived at the vet's office. Ken lifted Duchess out of the truck, and carried her through the front door. The veterinarian was shocked when he saw her; actually speechless.

"We know she is very old," Ken smiled, placing her gently on the floor. "But we are not sure how old." He related the story of how they found her.

The veterinarian examined her. She was twenty-eight inches tall at the shoulder and across her back she measured about two inches! "Just bones and hair," he mumbled. "She has to be at least eight or nine, I figure."

"What are you feeding her?" he asked, without taking his hands or his attention off Duchess.

Joanne explained, "I thought she seemed dehydrated so I have been giving her electrolytes plus any foods we could get her to eat."

"She's not dehydrated now. Is she eating?" Joanne nodded. "Why, then, did you bring her in?"

"I wanted to find out about that rear leg. And, maybe shots?"

His hands continued a thorough exam of her left rear leg; manipulation of the joints, moving forward and back, examining the atrophied muscles. "Thank you," he said. And in the next few minutes he repeated himself a number of times. He took a deep breath, looked at Seablooms and said, "I believe this hip problem is due to being hit by a car and having no treatment for the injury." He stroked her frail body and again said, "Thank you."

"Why do you keep saying that?" Joanne asked.

"Thank you for rescuing this grand old lady." The vet stroked her body once more, then stood, smiling down at Duchess.

Eventually Duchess gained weight and became the beautiful Newfoundland the Seablooms had dreamed of. Joanne exercised and massaged her hind leg until the muscle tone returned and she rarely limped anymore. She was a member of their family for eighteen happy months and died in her sleep one December morning.

CHAPTER THREE

Contact!

"What's your problem?" Ken queried.

Her eyes met his for a long time before she spoke.

"The first thing I saw when I opened my eyes this morning was the . . . empty chesterfield." An involuntary sniff. "I can still hear Brock's voice as if he just came running into the room and spoke those awful words, 'Mummy, Duchess died'."

Silence.

The rocking chair squeaked softly and rhythmically as Ken swallowed some more coffee, and waited, sensing that she still had things to say.

"We've lost animals before. This is the same kind of heart-break I felt when we put Kobe to sleep. Why does it have to hurt so much?" She was frustrated at her own feelings.

"It's been weeks since she died. I know Duchess was old. I thought she was healthy! She had a nice supper. And then, suddenly, she was gone," her voice trailed into a whisper.

Ken stood. He set his mug down on the coffee table and crossed the room to her side. He put his warm hand on Joanne's shoulder. With a gentle squeeze he shared her misery. "We all miss her, she was a special Newfoundland."

A few days later, before Ken rolled out of bed, Joanne heard, "I'm tired of not having a dog!"

She looked at him in sleepy surprise.

"It's just not the same around here since Duchess died," Ken blurted his feelings. "We know there aren't many Newfs around this area, but we need a dog."

Joanne stared at the ceiling as she thought about the past. They never gave up looking for a Newfoundland. It had become a way of life.

She reminded him, "You know I've talked to breeders and that's out! Every time I got my hands on a paper I checked the ads. I read you everything I found. We wanted a companion for her so badly. Now we don't even have one Newf, let alone two."

She pulled the covers over her face trying to blot out her emptiness.

"Yes, I know, there just weren't any!" Ken spoke to her still covered face. "Since we can't find another Newfoundland, perhaps we should look at other breeds."

Ken watched closely for her reaction.

Joanne pushed the covers back and glared at her husband, wondering how he could say that. She sat up in bed, brushed her long hair behind her ear with her fingers and hugged her knees with her arms. Her head moved slowly from side to side, but she said nothing.

"You aren't going to give up, are you?" he tested.

Joanne took a quick breath, fought back the tears that were just brimming in her eyes, and looked across the king size waterbed at her husband.

"She was here for only a year and a half, Ken, how could we learn to love her so much? I thought I was getting used to the idea of her being gone, but look at me . . .!" She struggled to finish her sentence and fell silent.

"You know it takes time," Ken whispered as he rolled out of bed and stood looking out the window. Tears also blurred his view of their tree-lined driveway.

"I think you need another dog. Actually, I think we all need another dog. I know the boys miss Duchess as much as we do. And, I believe we have to search even harder," Ken stated very emphatically, paused, then continued. He knew there would be no other dog but a Newfoundland. "I believe you will be happier if your mind is on the future and not the past!"

Joanne's mind raced back through the three years of the dedicated search to find Duchess and later the impossible task of finding a companion for her. Any time Joanne had seen a newspaper she automatically turned to the classified ads and to the SPCA column. It had been so frustrating. There was no animal shelter in their little town of Mission. She had contacted the Newfoundland Club and various rescue organizations. Phone calls to various shelters had always yielded the same response, "It is rare that a Newfoundland is available for adoption. Just keep checking back."

Ken vented his anger. "I'll tell you one thing, you are going to have to stop volunteering for the SPCA! It's costing us a fortune to care for these animals. And ever since that Pitbull was dropped off and killed forty of your rabbits, I've had it with rescue!"

Joanne thought about the time and energy she devoted to the rescue service. It was heartbreaking to deal with the endless supply of homeless animals. "That's okay by me. The boys need me and besides, with all those rabbits and five horses I have plenty to do. It's just too hard to resist some of those appealing faces and wagging tails, and know they have no one."

This was a big decision for Joanne. Ken listened carefully. This time she sounded really serious!

"We did love Kobe," he reminisced. "She was only a Husky-mix, not a Newf, but she was great to have around."

Joanne hopped out of bed. "Yes!" she blurted out, "and I remember that beautiful Siberian Husky we saw at the SPCA the time we stopped on the way to your Mum's. I remember how tempted we were and how worried I was about it. Then I called to make sure it got adopted in the next two days so they wouldn't put it to sleep." She shuddered. "I don't want to look at homeless dogs anymore, Ken. I just want a Newf."

Emotions rekindled frustrations.

"Remember when I found the ad for the Newf, free to a good home? I was so excited." Quietly she reflected. "When the lady answered the phone I was told that he'd already been re-homed. I was devastated. I gave her my phone number just in case it didn't work out." Joanne sighed. "That was so disappointing."

With a resurgence of commitment, she looked at her husband and said, "No, Ken, we will have no other kind of dog. We agreed, we both wanted another Newfoundland."

The days blended into weeks. Joanne continued to scan the classified ads. She knew the chances were slim. But since they still couldn't afford to buy a puppy, this was their only alternative.

Some time later the Seablooms were in North Vancouver on a visit to Ken's Mum. Ken and the boys were saying goodbye and on their way out the door. Joanne was, as usual, reading the ads.

"Ken! Wait! Ken, listen to this," she called, waving the newspaper toward him. "It's a Pet Corner ad in the local newspaper. The ad is for pets needing adoption through Pets Unlimited!" She was nearly breathless with excitement as she read out loud, "Ready for adoption, two Golden Retrievers, a Doberman, a Dachshund mix, and a male Newfoundland!"

Ken came back into the house, with the boys close behind. He took the paper, read the ad, and handed it back to Joanne. With a half-smile on his face he suggested, "You'd better give them a call."

22

She dialed up the number listed in the paper. The line was busy. Again and again, she dialed, but couldn't get through.

"Joanne, we really have to go," Ken said. "You've been trying for over a half-hour. We have an hour drive and we need to get home. You have animals to take care of."

Reluctantly, she hung up the receiver and smiled at Ken's Mum. "I know he is right, we'd better go." Then to Ken, "Okay, but maybe we can stop at a pay phone on the way home and I can try again."

"Sure," he smiled, as he said goodbye again and ushered the boys out the door ahead of him.

One final try before she joined them. The line was still busy. She grimaced her frustration and hung up the phone. "We'll keep you posted," she smiled to the boys' Grandmother as she rushed to join her family.

"I'm beginning to think the phone is off the hook," Ken said, as he backed their truck out of the driveway and they started home.

Perhaps he was correct, because the next stop at a pay phone along the way issued the same result, a busy signal.

"There, Ken, there is another phone, over there. There's even a place to pull in," Joanne pointed.

Ken pulled over for the second time. Joanne was out of the car before it came to a complete stop, holding her handful of change. She dialed up the number again, this time from memory and BINGO!

A woman's voice announced, "Pets Unlimited."

"I can't believe I really got you," Joanne said, "I've been trying for ages." The lady said something she couldn't understand. "Please, I can't hear you. I am at a pay phone at the busiest intersection in Vancouver. There is so much traffic, I am having a hard time hearing you. Please tell me, is the New-foundland dog still available?" She inhaled a deep catch-up breath, and felt herself squeezing the phone in her hand. It seemed the woman would never answer!

"Yes, the Newfoundland is still available. He is a neutered male. But you'll have to wait until tomorrow for details, please. You see, he is not with me. I am a volunteer today to answer the phone. I will have to contact the family who is taking care of him," the voice said. She seemed hesitant.

"Can you tell me, ah . . ." Joanne's mind was racing with excitement. "Is the dog here in the Vancouver area?" Traffic roared by. She found herself almost yelling into the phone, as though the lady would have trouble hearing her. "You see, we are here from out of town, and if the dog is close by we could see him today. It would be so helpful," she urged.

"I'm so sorry, dear," the voice tried to be loud and strong to be sure Joanne could hear. "Henry is on the Sechelt Peninsula in a foster home. We'll have to contact the family and call you back."

Joanne felt a twinge of panic. Someone else might get to him first. "Has anyone else called about him today?" she inquired, fearful they would miss out on the opportunity.

"Not to worry, dear," the lady said, loud and clear over the din of the traffic. "Now, give me your phone number and I will contact you in the morning as soon as I have been in touch with Henry's foster family."

Joanne gave her phone number slowly and distinctly. "Thank you, I'll be waiting to hear from you," she said. With a very empty feeling in the pit of her stomach she clicked down the receiver and headed for the truck.

"What'd they say, Mom, can we have a new dog? Is it a boy

or a girl?" Dirk and Brock introduced a chorus of questions. Their excitement filled the air.

"Oh, Ken, the dog is available! But she would tell me nothing but that! He is in a foster home on the Peninsula." Joanne hopped into the truck and pulled the door shut. "I don't know how I can wait until tomorrow! It's a male. She called him Henry. She has to talk to his foster family and then she will call us tomorrow with more information." Then she turned to Ken with a strange expression on her face, "Funny thing, she said 'not to worry' when I asked if anyone else had called about him."

Ken smiled as he pulled away from the curb and into the traffic. This should be an interesting trip home, he thought. He turned to Joanne and smiled. "I guess we will have to believe her," he said. "We can wait until morning. Just think of how long we have waited up until now!"

The boys started talking and laughing. Joanne's mind was a blur of excitement and a million questions. Finally all four were picking out new names for a dog they didn't even know. Gradually, they grew quieter and Ken whistled softly to himself most of the way home.

CHAPTER FOUR

Ring! Telephone! Ring!

Joanne opened her eyes. Suddenly she was wide-awake. The sun streaked across the bedroom and against the far wall. It was morning! She sat up and checked the clock, it was nearly 7:00 A.M. Today they would hear from Pets Unlimited. The lady said she would call with more information about the Newf. Joanne's body quivered with a rush of excitement.

She hopped out of bed, pulled on her jeans and a sweatshirt and hurried out to feed the animals. It was early. She knew she could finish outside and get back in the house before the phone call came through.

At the back door she pulled on her gumboots and made her way across the grassy yard toward the barn. Even before she got there, the animals heard her approach. The Arabian gelding and Buddy Boy, her ancient Shetland pony, greeted her with soft nickers. That alerted the rest of the crew. The Miniature horse mare, Sassy came trotting in from the corral. Her young foal, Cameo, came bouncing along behind. Sunshine knew the signals and rushed to join in.

All of the animals' ears perked forward in anticipation. There were more soft nickers, and a general rustling around for position. The crew eagerly awaited their morning grain and a few leaves of hay.

Phaedran, the Arabian, pushed his way in for a hands-on greeting. "Good morning, old boy," Joanne crooned. "How's my best friend this morning?" His big head pushed forward to her so she could massage behind his ears and along the side of his neck.

As she performed this morning ritual, she realized for the moment that she had put aside the anxiety of waiting for the phone call. The aromas of warm horse bodies and the sweet fragrance of green hay had a therapeutic effect on her mind and body.

With a final pat to Phaedran's neck, she greeted each of her animals with gentle contact. Her experienced hands touched and glided over a neck, back and rump, or quickly massaged between the eyes. Each animal had its own preference. There was special attention to the young ones. Already they knew the pleasure of her gentle hands. She finished up barn chores and headed for the rabbit shed.

Show rabbits of many kinds thumped around in their cages with excitement as she appeared. She doled out morning rations of food and water to French and English Angoras, Netherland Dwarfs and Mini Lops.

Joanne checked her watch. It was eight thirty! The lady could call at any moment! "Bye bunnies," she said as she hurried to finish up the cages, then headed toward the house. She felt some guilt at not giving them more individual attention, but not this morning! She needed to get back to the house.

The sun felt good on her back. The sky was deep blue, a sight not always evident in southwestern British Columbia. Today looked like a really good day!

As she kicked off her boots at the back porch she looked around their one-acre world. There were sprawling blackberry bushes forming a fence row; honeysuckle contributed a morning fragrance. It made her smile. She liked it here. It was a nice place for the boys to play and grow up and it would be even

28

better when there was a Newf around the place again. She opened the door and joined Ken in the kitchen.

"Hi, the phone didn't ring, did it?" She felt her anxiety level rising again.

Ken shook his head, "Nope, not yet."

Actually it was a little early, she told herself as she started to fix breakfast for her hungry boys. There was an air of excitement as they talked and ate. The thought of having a big furry friend around again generated good feelings. The conversation turned to thoughts of Duchess. It was an important time for the boys, especially, because they expressed their feelings of missing her. Joanne was surprised. She did not realize how important the dog was to Dirk and Brock.

"Remember, boys, he won't be like Duchess," their Mum reminded them. "He might be just as nice, but he will be different. He might be bigger; he might run around a lot. I'll bet he will like to chase a ball and splash in the turtle pond." Anticipation and laughter filled their morning. When breakfast was over, the boys went to do their chores. Time began to drag.

"It's nearly one o'clock," Joanne chewed on her lip. It was a sure sign of her frustration. "I expected that lady to call by now. She has our phone number. I gave it to her carefully."

Ken agreed. "The only thing I can figure is that they had trouble getting a hold of the foster home family. There is not a lot we can do but wait, Joanne."

So wait they did, all day long, and all day the next day. There was no phone call! Lack of response was taking its toll on the whole family. Finally Joanne could not be patient any longer. Haunted by the feeling that they had missed out on yet another Newf, she dialed up the number from the newspaper once more.

"I thought we would hear from you by now," she started.

"It's about the male Newfoundland that was in the Vancouver paper," she stated breathlessly.

"I spoke with a lady a few days ago and we haven't heard a word! She said she would . . ."

"Oh, yes, you spoke with me. I was still waiting for some more information on him," she interrupted. "His name is Henry and he is a neutered male. I do know that much. I really don't think you need to worry about losing out on him," she reassured, "he has been looking for a home for two years!"

Joanne's mind raced. Why didn't we hear about him before now? She wondered. Why would any Newfoundland have trouble finding a home? For two years!

The woman interrupted Joanne's thoughts as she confessed, "I was also worried about how we would get him to you. He is on the Sechelt Peninsula. You are quite far away."

"No problem," Joanne laughed, "we would come and get him! We can combine the trip with a visit to my parents. They live in Gibsons. It is only a ferry ride and a few kilometers beyond."

"That would be most helpful, yes it would." The woman sounded relieved. "Now, I do have to contact the foster home. And, as soon as I touch base with them, I will let you know," she reassured.

"Oh, thanks! You know, we can hardly wait to hear from you. It is so hard to find a Newfoundland, almost impossible. We are so anxious to give him a home." Joanne was babbling and she realized it. "Please call us as soon as you know. We'll be waiting."

CHAPTER FIVE

This is Henry

The alarm issued a five A.M. wake-up call. Joanne was out of bed and pulling on her jeans in an instant. "Oh, Ken," she said to her snoozing husband, "it's Saturday!" Her voice bubbled with anticipation. "The day is finally here. We are going to get our Newfoundland." As she buttoned her blouse and looked out the window, the first light of morning was in the eastern sky. She was wired!

"We are going to meet Henry," she sang in a silly voice, then leaned over and gave her husband a kiss on the top of his head. "I'll go start breakfast while you get the boys up, okay?"

Ken inhaled a deep wake-up breath. "Sure," he blinked. He shared Joanne's excitement. As she disappeared out the door she heard Ken's voice reminding her, "Ferry leaves at 7:20 A.M."

Soon they were all eating cold cereal. Ken and Dirk had peanut butter spread on their toast. Brock and Joanne preferred blackberry jam, from their very own berry bushes in the side yard.

The conversation was as sweet as their blackberry jam. Won't it be fun to have a Newfoundland on the floor to step over again! The boys planned how they would play ball with him. Ken thought of the black furry coat he loved to ruffle with his hands, and how nice it would be to have a big dog just to walk by his side. Joanne wondered about his face. What would he look like? It had been too long since there was a Newfoundland presence in her life.

"Come on boys, get in the truck, we are ready to go!" Joanne's voice was full of excitement. It echoed the feelings deep inside her. "We have to be there on time, because that ferry won't wait for us!"

The motor purred smoothly during the little warm-up.

"Everybody ready?" Ken asked, checking the smiling faces in the rear view mirror. He glanced over at Joanne. She was sitting there with a big grin on her face.

"I thought this weekend would never come!" she puffed, still out of breath from her rushed morning doing animal chores. "Ken, can you believe it, we are going to look at a Newf?" Then, after a thoughtful silence, " I'll bet anything we bring him home. I just have a feeling about this," she nodded.

Ken looked over at her and smiled. "Yeah, me too. I believe we are going to get our Newfie. I tossed a couple of blankets in the back for him." He pulled out of the driveway smiling to himself.

That statement drew a surprised glance from his front seat companion. She had always been the accepting one of the two. Her favorite response for unusual situations, "It's just meant to be, Ken." Usually he would scoff and add some chiding remark. This time, he *agreed* with her? Today, there was no doubt in their minds. This dog was waiting for them.

"Are we almost to the ferry, Daddy?" Six- year old Dirk questioned from the back seat. They had been on the road for about fifteen minutes. Still ahead were a one-hour drive to the Port at Horseshoe Bay and the forty-minute ferry crossing. Henry's foster family lived in Robert's Creek. That was another forty minute drive.

"It'll be a while, boys. It's still a long way to the ferry," Ken sighed. Then, to alleviate boredom, "What do you suppose the

Newf is doing right now?" Brock thought he would be sleeping. "Playing ball, I think he's playing ball," said Dirk.

"You boys remember, Henry isn't used to kids. So, don't jump around and hang on him. He will like you better if you don't get crazy," Joanne reminded them.

"Mummy," Brock asked thoughtfully, "can Henry go to the restaurant with us, and have a hamburger?"

"Not this trip. Remember, we are going to Nana's and Grand-dad's house," Joanne smiled, amused at her four year olds' request. "Nana is fixing us a nice big lunch."

The boys dozed off and it was quiet in the truck. A medley of Van Halen songs pulsed from the tape deck as Ken's thumbs kept time on the steering wheel.

Joanne was lost in her own thoughts as the distance between them and the ferry shortened. "I'm disappointed that Henry isn't younger," she admitted, "five and a half isn't young."

"You're right," Ken agreed. "I want to make darn sure he is in good health. It's so much easier and less expensive to have a healthy pet. It is hard on both of us to lose one like we lost Kobe."

Ken's statement took Joanne back to her childhood and poor sickly Wispy. She remembered the vet's expression when she carried the little pup into the office. It would have been so much more fun if Wispy had been healthy. Lot's of vet bills! She had learned so much about animal care during those months, working to pay off those bills. Caring for animals is expensive!

"...anything about the adoption agreement?" Ken's voice stirred her back to the present.

"Hm?" Joanne inquired. In her mind she was far away; many years and experiences ago. Her memory had her at the aquarium shop somewhere between trimming a birds beak and fixing a broken bird leg when she heard Ken's voice.

"The adoption agreement," Joanne, "didn't the volunteer on the phone say she would mail us the agreement to look at and sign if we agreed to take Henry?" Ken reminded her, "it never came."

"I'm sure the foster home people will have one for us. The adoption takes place there," she mused. "Those papers all look pretty much alike."

"Hey boys, wake up! There's the first sign to the ferry. It won't be long now," Ken said from the driver's seat. "It's going to be a pretty day along the coast, and a nice ride across the water."

The boys got wiggly with excitement. "We'll have a good time on the ferry," their dad encouraged, "it's the same one we take to visit Nana and Grand dad." He could feel his own spirits lift as their adventure became more of a reality.

"Look, boys, you can see the ocean!" Joanne pointed to a silvery gray patch of light in the distance.

The early morning coastal fog was lifting. Occasional shafts of sunlight streaked through the thinning layer of clouds. It teased the travelers with promises of a blue-sky day, then disappeared.

The crossing was fun for the boys. Once on board the big ferry, they left the truck on a lower level and scurried up the stairs and onto an inside deck where they could sit in comfort and safety and watch through a window. The ferry moved gently up and down over the powerful surface swells, out of Horseshoe Bay and into the Georgia Straight.

Joanne and Ken watched the ferry terminal come closer into view. "Somewhere over there, our Newfoundland is waiting for us, Ken," she whispered in her excitement. "We're coming, Henry, we're coming."

Chapter Five

The view of Langdale grew larger on the horizon. When the dock was in full view, Ken mustered his little crew. "Back in the truck, boys, we are almost ready to dock."

"I want to watch, Daddy," insisted Dirk.

"Not this time, son, we have to go down and get in our truck. We want to be all ready when they open the ramp. Come on, Henry's waiting." Ken's enthusiasm was almost childlike. "Let's go find our dog."

The Sechelt Peninsula is located northwest of Vancouver, British Columbia and accessible by ferry. The Georgia Straight to the west of the peninsula is dotted with small islands. The aroma of salt air was a special treat to the Seablooms whose home in Mission is far back from the sea. From the Port at Langdale it wasn't far to the growing town of Gibsons, where the boys grand parents lived. This area of the mainland is heavily forested and dotted with many Provincial Parks.

The truck rumbled off the ferry, down a clanking metal ramp and on to the solid ground.

"Okay, Joanne, you navigate. I know Robert's Creek is straight out the highway through Gibsons. After we get there you will have to give me the details," Ken sounded like a man on a mission.

Joanne did as he requested. She handed the boys a snack to occupy the last leg of their journey.

"Ken, you passed Mum's and Dad's road!" She looked at him in surprise.

"We'll go see the dog first," he looked at her and smiled. "I don't want to take a chance on someone else getting there first!"

"Suits me," she chuckled as she reached in her pocket. "Got our map." She smiled at the boys and waved it in the air. "Henry's foster family gave me good directions over the phone."

Joanne looked up to see that they were now in a completely wooded area. Cedar trees, high underbrush and areas of lacey ferns were a beautiful sight as the occasional sun shone through on to bright patches of green.

"We are almost there," she whispered as she studied the map. The big green mailboxes with many lock compartments stood in plain view. "Go right, down that road," she directed.

"There Ken, there's the driveway!" Joanne's heart was thumping as she pointed to the entrance obscured by shrubs. "This is the place!"

"I think she said their name is McMannis, McIntyre, something like that. I was so excited I hardly listened to anything but directions." Joanne was not happy with herself. She should have written down their name.

"Those gates look homemade," Ken mused as he pulled off the road and stopped at the barred entrance.

"She said to just punch the buzzer when we got to the gate," Joanne reminded him as she hopped out of the truck and buzzed their arrival.

A slender lady with dark brown hair came down the road in a rush and welcomed the Seablooms. "Hi," she was smiling, "I'm Marty McMartin. You must be the Seablooms. Drive right on in! I'll meet you at the house."

The road made a slight curve and continued into the property. The McMartin's home, surrounded by trees, was not visible at first. Ken pulled in and parked near the small rustic cabin.

As the Seablooms got out of their car, Joanne reminded the boys once more not to get too excited around a dog that they didn't know.

Both Ken and Joanne noticed what appeared to be a New-foundland chained to the side of the building. Their eyes met.

Before they could say anything they were greeted by a huge Great Pyrenees.

At the same moment, Marty hurried up the drive. "It's okay, he's friendly," she smiled.

Marty's husband stepped off the porch, "Hi, I'm Jim. You've had quite a journey already this morning." He greeted them with a warm handshake, including the boys.

The lady poured a dish full of kibble from a bag on the front porch, then turned to the Seablooms.

"Come, let's have you take a look at the Newfoundland," she said as she hurried them around the corner of the cabin.

The dog greeted all of them with a happy face and a wagging tail. Marty turned to them, smiling.

"This is Henry!"

CHAPTER SIX

We Have Our Newf!

The Seablooms gathered around Henry as he looked up at them with his happy face. He tugged hard on his chain and his big bushy tail wagged exuberantly from side to side. He was obviously a people lover!

He's not very big for a Newf, Joanne mused, as she began her critique of the hairy creature. Both ears were clean. His coat was shining and healthy. No skin problems, she thought, as she brushed back his coat on his shoulders and his hindquarters. She was truly impressed with his honest, outgoing nature.

The boys were all over him, touching and laughing. Brock put his head down on Henry's neck. "Mummie, he feels like Duchess, all warm," he exclaimed.

Marty unhooked his chain and immediately he disappeared around to the front of the cabin. "He isn't running away," she laughed, "he's looking for something to eat. He has a great appetite. He is going to check his food dish."

The family followed her around to the front of the cabin. They gathered around Henry as he eagerly gobbled up his ration of food, his tail was still wagging all the time. The boys moved close enough to pat him as he ate and he seemed to enjoy the attention. The Seablooms watched carefully. They were relieved to see that Henry showed absolutely no aggression.

"You are very trusting," Marty observed.

"He is a Newfoundland," Joanne announced with confidence and a smile. "He looks as though he has a very stable temperament."

"So far, so good," Ken whispered to Joanne.

They stood near the porch watching the boys and Henry get acquainted. Marty handed his paperwork to Joanne. The records included vaccine dates, a rabies certificate, and a birth date. The McMartins exchanged worried glances and watched intently as the Seablooms studied the information.

"He has just had his teeth cleaned," Marty interrupted a bit too loudly, " I don't think that is included in those records."

She added nervously as the Seablooms continued to read, "You really do need to keep them brushed."

"Look at this, Ken, this record says he was born on December 6, 1980!" Joanne pointed to the date. She grappled with her feelings as she did the math in her head.

"The date of birth on this record means that he is really seven and a half! Is this true?" she asked, as she turned to the couple with astonishment written on her face.

Jim looked at his wife, indicating she would respond. Her face was completely free of any visible emotion. There was a moment of complete silence, then Marty looked Joanne straight in the eyes and said, "Yes, it's true. Henry is really seven and a half. He has been looking for a home for two years! But," she paused, "he is *such* a nice dog, and I was afraid you wouldn't come to look at him if you knew his true age."

The woman did not apologize for her actions. "I hope you aren't angry," she continued. "I know that Newfoundlands don't live a lot longer than eight or nine, but I want him to have a good home for however long he lives. He really is a dear dog."

She ruffled his ears and gave him a few strokes down his back.

"His life has really been very sad," she offered. She began relating the facts of his life as the Seablooms listened intently.

"Henry was born on Galiano Island. We know that a young couple bought him when he was a puppy. When their marriage broke up she kept the dog. Apparently Henry was lonely and started to wander while she was at work. Eventually he just disappeared! Ads and posters were put up all around and everyone in the area was on the lookout for him. Six months later he turned up sixty miles away!"

She was quiet for a moment, then continued. "We know all about his life except that six month period. He seemed to be living on his own, right out in the middle of the forest! When he turned up he was in good condition except for a matted coat. Ever since then Henry has remained in foster care."

Joanne felt sympathy for the happy-faced Henry as she watched the boys patting him.

"I can't understand why he had so many foster homes. He seems like a good dog." She was searching for answers.

"Many different volunteers tried. There is just no fence that could hold him! You know how we foster home families are. We do the best we can with each animal that comes to us. He never went to a real adoptive family, just temporary homes because he kept running away. In his last foster home the lady worked full time and he wandered, just like with his first family."

Marty looked at her husband and continued. "That is why you saw him on a chain. Even though our place is fenced we are afraid that he will not stay unless he is on a chain."

Jim nodded his agreement.

Joanne walked over to Henry and patted him gently on his side.

"Sounds like he was never really happy wherever he was. He just kept moving on, as if he were searching but could never make a connection."

"That's our Henry, alright," Jim responded, nodding his head in affirmation.

Marty spoke kindly of him, yet with some frustration. The Seablooms could hear it in her voice. Both Ken and Joanne got the feeling that she was almost desperate for them to go through with the adoption.

Joanne looked at Ken, "I wonder why we never heard of him. I thought we had covered all the bases." She shrugged.

"This brings up a very important point," Jim stated with a calm, almost rehearsed statement. "As a part of this adoption you will have to agree to keep Henry on a chain."

Joanne listened in disbelief. "I don't understand. That is usually a No-no," was her definitive answer. "I've worked with enough Humane Societies, and SPCA's to know that this is strictly against adoption policies!" She continued. "The lady I spoke with on the phone said she would mail me a contract but it never came."

"No contract," the man affirmed. He read frustration on Joanne's face. " I assure you it will be okay. Everyone knows what Henry is like. You just have to promise to keep him tied."

First impressions of Henry chained to the side of the cabin popped back into Joanne's head. She felt sad. The thought of taking him home and tying him up in their world made her feel sick in the pit of her stomach.

However, the reality of having a Newfoundland of their very own suppressed any other emotion she had. Since the McMartins were comfortable with the idea of tying him, Joanne had few misgivings. She knew that in a few days he would settle in and it wouldn't be necessary anymore.

Without talking to Ken about it, she heard herself saying, "I guess we don't really have a choice."

Ken nodded that it would be fine with him. "We can make him a nice long slider."

They both wanted to take him home right away. The slider seemed a perfect way to control him while they "Henry-proofed" their fences. Ken and Joanne were pretty sure that the volunteers were exaggerating about his strong will.

The whole adoption event took about one half-hour. They made their verbal commitment and the seven-year-old Newfoundland was theirs.

Joanne scribbled their names and phone number on a scrap of paper and handed it to the couple.

"Here, just in case you need to contact us," she smiled.

"I guess we are ready to go then." Ken directed his words to the couple.

They smiled and nodded in agreement.

"Please keep in touch. I do want this dog to be happy and have a family to love him," Marty gave Henry a final pat.

"Come on boys, let's see if Henry would like to go for a ride," Ken called as he opened the back doors of his truck. Henry was right there. He jumped in, pushed aside the blankets and lay down. His happy face indicated to all that he was ready, even eager, for his next adventure.

"Everyone in?" Ken queried. He turned the key and the engine purred softly as he turned to Joanne and smiled.

"We have our Newf!" Joanne whispered, as tears of joy slipped down her face.

Ken glanced at Henry in the rear view mirror as he guided the truck down the drive. He looked at the boys and again at his wife. He was driving a truck full of happy faces.

Marty ran down the drive after them, waving her arm.

"Oh! By the way, don't let Henry near cats!"

And so began a new era for both the Seablooms and a Newfoundland named Henry.

CHAPTER SEVEN

Welcome Home Henry!

Ken opened the windows in the truck canopy to give Henry plenty of fresh air. Joanne and the boys watched just in case their new dog decided to jump through the screens. It was soon evident that he enjoyed the ride. His ears flopped in the breeze that was coming through the window. His nose tested the air as it delivered messages about the world outside the truck.

"Nana and Grand-dad will like our new dog," Dirk proclaimed from the back seat.

"You are right. I can hardly wait to show him off." Joanne's voice was full of enthusiasm.

This was a dream come true for the whole family. She looked back at Henry again and felt such a special joy. He was their Newfoundland!

Henry was on his feet as the truck slowed and pulled to a stop at the Bonniebrook home of Joanne's parents. Nana's yard was beautiful. The lawn and flowers surrounded a pretty little white cottage that was perched on a cliff above the ocean.

Henry sensed the smell of the salt water. This was new territory for him and the old experienced roamer was extremely curious.

He hopped out of the truck with his tail wagging and greeted Joanne's parents.

After a few minutes of getting acquainted, Joanne attached his chain to a nearby apple tree as she explained to them about the promise they made to the foster family.

Her Mum had lunch all ready to serve. They brought it outside and the whole family ate, sitting with Henry. They later tried
a short visit inside. Constant pacing, panting and restlessness
were strong reminders that he had never been a housedog.

After a short visit they said their good-byes. Grandparents
got their hugs, and the Seabloom family headed home with their
furry treasure. They made the forty-five-minute ferry crossing,
then the hour drive to Mission, with an occasional stop along the
way for "dog walking." It was evening by the time Henry arrived
at his new home.

"I know the property is fully fenced, Ken, but we did promise. This will be for just a few days until he gets used to us."
Joanne's expression clearly revealed her distaste for what she
had agreed to do.

The boys watched as Joanne reluctantly put Henry on his
chain. Her eyes filled with tears as she stood looking down at
his adorable face. It seemed so wrong!

"Where's he going to sleep tonight?" Ken asked, eager to
move on to another subject.

Joanne blinked at him in surprise. "Gee, I hadn't given it a
thought. Too busy thinking of other stuff," she laughed. "How
about the empty bedroom?"

"We do want him to be a housedog. There's no time like
now to start," Ken reasoned.

"Okay. We can put papers on the floor and give him a blanket to sleep on. At least we will know he is safe!" She said.

She brought him a big pan of water and poured a bowl full
of kibble for his first meal as a Seabloom. The chain clanked
against the water bucket as he lapped up a big drink.

Joanne could hardly manage to look into his eyes. "I'd hate
for you to get loose and get hit by a car, old boy," she said as she

gave him a pat. With a sigh she turned and walked to the house. She still had other animals to care for.

"Come on boys, let's give Henry a little time alone to get used to things around here. He has had a busy day."

She watched Brock and Dirk giving Henry pats and a hug. "They really did miss Duchess," she thought.

When they brought Henry in for the night, they learned that he was not house broken. He thoroughly enjoyed pats and attention but clearly he was an outside dog!

Henry was not happy in his "guest" bedroom. He did not elect to keep it clean! Even a walk in the night didn't help. He waited until Joanne brought him back to his room, then again proceeded to "do his job." He definitely had a knack for being graphic about his dislike for indoor living!

"Morning will be better," Joanne told herself as she crawled back into bed.

When the new day began there was quite a crew of animals for Henry to meet. Joanne was anxious for them to get acquainted. There were cats and bunnies, some turtles and tropical fish, even pet mice and a guinea pig. In the barn and pasture, he would meet Phaedran, the Arabian gelding, some Miniature horses, and Buddy Boy, the old Shetland pony that was destined to become Henry's good friend.

"Come on, Henry, let's go meet the rest of your family," Joanne encouraged as she opened the door and stepped outside.

"No! You don't eat cats!" She mandated as she snapped on his leash.

Years of experience had formed other behaviors into this newcomer. Just as they came around the corner of the house, Henry exploded with energy. Joanne was airborne as the leash was ripped out of her hands.

Before she could catch up, "Mr. Strong Will and Determination" reached the hen house and ripped open the chicken wire. It took only a moment of confusion, then he charged through the fence and into the trees with a chicken in his jaws!

"Henry!" Then louder, "Henry!" Was he deaf? He paid absolutely no attention to Joanne's calls. She started over the fence after him. Scratched by blackberry bushes, frustrated and horrified, she watched. The Newfoundland was back through the fence and had another of her hens in his mouth.

These were her friends, her elderly pets! They all had special names. Henry was clearly out of control. All she could think of was protecting the rest of the flock, which she did while she screamed for Ken's help.

Henry ignored Joanne's frantic calls and disappeared again into the bush. Joanne followed him this time and found her poor little hens laid neatly side by side under a tree. It looked as if they were to be a future meal.

A very determined Joanne captured the chicken thief and this time she was not so reluctant to confine him to his chain. Ken made the repairs to the chicken coop.

Later that evening, Joanne looked at Ken. "Thanks for fixing the chicken coop. I'll see that it never happens again."

"You know, Ken," she said thoughtfully, "I believe that Henry had no idea that he was doing anything wrong. You should have seen him at work. He was fast, and he looked experienced. No wonder he survived in the wild. He certainly has the skills."

During the next few weeks all of the fences were rebuilt around their one-acre home. The Seablooms were to learn that, in spite of their efforts, the fences would never be strong enough!

Joanne looked up at the calendar one morning about two weeks after Henry came home. They still had not received a contract from the rescue group. It was after 9:00 A.M. Surely someone would be there.

She double-checked the original Pets Unlimited ad, picked up the phone and dialed up the number.

"Hello, I spoke with someone two weeks ago about a male Newfoundland that was ready for adoption."

"Oh, I am so sorry, dear, he has already been placed with a family. I hope you will . . ."

"Yes, I know," Joanne said with a smile. "We are the family that adopted him. I am calling because we still have not received a contract as you promised."

She questioned the lady about the requirement that they keep Henry confined to a chain.

The lady explained, "Oh, he's the exception to the rule." Her voice was confident and commanding. "When you receive the contract, just cross out that part with a pen." Joanne's mind processed the comment.

Her thoughts were interrupted by an anxious voice.

"You haven't let him loose, have you? He has been looking for a home for two years because he was not happy anywhere!" She tried hard to make her point. "If you give him freedom, he will be gone!"

Joanne explained that she and Ken had agreed to put him on a slider as a means of control. This seemed to satisfy the lady's fears.

"I will put the contract in the mail today, dear," she promised.

Later that evening Joanne related her conversation with the Pets' Unlimited volunteer. "I don't want to loose him, Ken. She said he will be gone if he is free. That scares me."

The next morning Ken went to work on Henry's slider. He

extended the length so that their new Newfoundland could come up the steps and into the house through the front door. Henry enjoyed the extended freedom and spent more time with his family.

Gradually, Henry learned to come when he was called. He obeyed sit and down commands. He even stopped trying to eat all of the farm critters. There was always food in his dish. Eventually he even stayed in the yard during the days without being on his slider. But at night, he was attached for his own safety.

Best of all, Henry was a part of the Seabloom family and he knew he was loved.

The wanderer has found his home.

CHAPTER EIGHT

Home In Mission

During that first summer with Seablooms, Henry became the center of their lives. He enjoyed trips to a nearby lake. He was a powerful swimmer and he never tired of retrieving sticks for the boys.

Joanne had an old pony cart she bought for the Miniature horses. She thought it might be just the right size for Henry. One day when the boys had a friend over to play, she decided to try it out.

"Come on Henry, you and I are going to give the boys a treat," Joanne encouraged, as the big dog patiently cooperated while he was hitched to a horse cart with a make-shift harness.

"You are a pretty strong old guy," she bragged to him as she attached a lead to his buckle collar. "I think I'll put your chain collar on too, just for a little extra control."

She attached the second lead and they were ready to go!

"Come on boys, Henry is going to take you for a ride."

This was an invitation they eagerly accepted. All three boys climbed aboard.

"Okay Henry, pull!" Joanne voiced her enthusiasm as he willingly moved forward. The boys giggled and laughed as the cart began to bounce over the bumpy surface.

"Hey, Mummy, this is fun!" Brock's voice vibrated his excitement as the others laughed their agreement.

"Good boy, Henry!" Joanne encouraged him as he began to lean into his harness. They moved out of the driveway and onto

51

the road.

Her two leads came in very handy as his confidence began to build. He exhibited natural talents as a draft dog. With his head held high he surged forward.

Henry started to trot. The boys giggled and laughed their encouragement. Faster and faster he trotted down the road! Things were out of control. Joanne couldn't keep up with the pace Henry set for himself.

As they went over the crest of a hill and started down the slope on the other side, Joanne was out of breath and realized she was in trouble. She knew she had to match his pace. Because of the boys she couldn't let go! Henry and the children were having a great time and Joanne was in a state of panic.

There was a gravel road ahead that turned off to the right. She had to slow him down! The boys were in danger. Her body felt like it was floating as she tried to keep up with him. Her mind raced for answers to solve her problem. She had to turn him onto that gravel road ahead, hoping it would bring the situation back under control.

With one hand firmly on each lead, she used all of her strength, pulling to the right. Henry got the message! He made the turn onto the gravel road! Reluctantly he slowed down and the cart finally came to a stop.

Henry was panting a little. "Good boy," Joanne whispered, as she gasped for breath.

The boys wanted to keep going!

"Why did you stop him?" was the unanimous chorus from the passengers, "We want to go more!"

Joanne was still breathing heavily and for a few moments she didn't answer. She looked at Henry. He was just as eager to keep moving as his passengers were. She gave him a firm snap on the lead, a reminder that he needed to be still.

"Just a minute boys," she urged, "I need time to rest. I didn't know Henry could go so fast!"

"You're huffing and puffing," they laughed at her. "Can we go some more, now?"

Henry waited as impatiently as the boys did for Joanne's signal.

"Hold on, boys," she cautioned. She felt ready to accept the challenge once again.

"Are you ready, Henry?"

She already knew the answer. "Easy, old man!" She commanded as she turned the dog toward home. Their journey was fun but much more controlled.

That evening Joanne shared the experience with Ken, who listened with characteristic acceptance. He never knew what to expect when Joanne said she had something to tell him.

"Henry's energy was incredible, Ken," Joanne pronounced, as she painted a vivid picture of the events of the afternoon.

"I can't believe that he is really as old as his records state." She shook her head in doubt. "I can tell you for sure, never again will he get hitched to anything with wheels on it!"

Ken looked at her and laughed. She certainly had a knack for causing excitement with her animals.

"Why don't you double check the information they gave us, Joanne. That should help to clear things up."

The next morning she made two calls of inquiry.

"Hello, we have a rescue dog we got from you about a month ago. I want to check on the records that came with him," Joanne began, speaking to Gail from the placement service.

"I will be glad to help if I can," the voice responded. "Tell me about your dog."

"His name is Henry, he is a Newfoundland . . ." Joanne was interrupted.

"You still have Henry?" The volunteer was elated! "That is wonderful! How is he doing?"

"He is just fine," Joanne assured her. "As a matter of fact, he is so strong and healthy, we can not believe he is really as old as his records indicate. Will you double check for us with information that you have there?"

"Yes, I'd be glad to," she responded. "Actually, I practically know them by heart, we have worked with him for so long. Can you hold for just a moment?"

"Be glad to," was Joanne's positive response.

Five years, Joanne thought, I'll bet that Marty McMartin was right when she told us that over the phone. Henry could not possibly be seven and a half.

"Mrs. Seabloom? You are his adoptive family, right?"

"Yes," said Joanne

"I am holding his original paperwork in my hand. It says his date of birth is December 6, 1980. Is there anything else I can help you with?" was the volunteer's cordial response.

"No, not just now, thanks," Joanne said, "except that we love him dearly and we enjoy him so much. Thank you."

His original owner was next. This was a bit more difficult.

Joanne worried as she dialed up the number. She wasn't exactly sure what she was going to say. The phone was ringing. It was easier than she expected.

"I felt so bad for him, but I had to let him go. There was really no option." The young woman's voice was confident. "I am truly glad to hear from you and know he is happy. I have thought of Henry from time to time and wondered how he was."

Joanne explained her reason for calling and listened with some fascination to her brief response.

"Henry came from a litter of thirteen. They all lived. I think he was about seven weeks old when we got him. I remember the first summer we had him, we went to a party for the whole litter when the pups were six month old. It was so much fun. All the other people loved his name, Henry 1st. That was the summer of 1981," she related.

"Then, after our divorce, I was at work all the time and I know Henry was lonely. He wouldn't stay home."

"His birthday?" Joanne inquired, "Do you remember when he was born?"

"Oh, yes," she laughed, "Sorry. His birthday was December 6, 1980."

Joanne thanked her and the conversation was over.

I guess we are just very lucky, she thought, as she hung up the phone; lucky he is healthy, unlucky he is so old.

During that first winter, Henry used his strength and exuberance to pull the boys up and down the snow-covered road on a sled or plastic bag. He took Joanne on a few joy rides as well. She continued to be amazed at this Newfoundland. He was full of energy and never got tired!

One summer day when Henry was eight years old, he and Joanne were sitting on the front porch together. A car pulled up in the driveway. The car door opened and a lady walked toward them. She appeared to have no fear of the big dog sitting with Joanne.

"Hello," she said, "I am from the pound and I am out checking licenses on the local dogs." She came closer. "Do you have one for your Newfie?"

Joanne had to be honest. "No, we don't." She smiled and continued. "He is very old. We took him as a rescue dog. I really don't expect to have him much longer."

Henry watched, but didn't move.

"I drive by here a lot and I have seen him before," she said as she took a closer look at the dog beside Joanne.

"That might have been Duchess," Joanne suggested. Then she went on to explain that she, too had been very old and had died about Christmas time.

The woman moved closer.

"Yes, I can see he has quite a gray muzzle," she said, "You're probably right. It's not likely you will have him much longer. But you really do need to buy a license."

Joanne thought about the expense. She leaned over and ruffled Henry's neck.

"Would you ask your boss if this is really necessary?"

"Sure, I can do that. I have no idea what he will say." She turned to go. As she got in her car she said, "I will leave a note in your mailbox if you have to get one."

"Thanks." Joanne smiled and waved as the lady started to back out the driveway.

The car slowed and stopped. The driver pulled back up the drive near the porch, but didn't get out of her car. She called out the window to Joanne, "I want to thank you. You are the first person all day that has been nice to me." Then she waved goodbye and left.

When she was gone, Joanne turned to go in the house. In the window sat Maxzi, their little white poodle, very visible during the whole conversation!

Joanne never found a message in her mailbox from the pound.

Over the years, Henry never lost his cheerful exuberance. Gradually, he started to tire more easily after a game of fetch. He no longer was allowed to pull the sled. Like she promised, never again did he pull that cart! He still loved to swim and retrieve sticks.

Henry could always find a new way to occupy his time and entertain the Seabloom family. On one side of the front yard there was a run for Joanne's flock of Silky Bantam chickens. A friend stopped in one day with a little gift.

"Joanne, I just rescued this poor little hen off the highway! Look how tiny she is! Now, you know I don't raise anything but purebreds," she laughed, "and I know you get critters of all kinds dumped on you frequently. Will you take this little one? I just couldn't leave her out there alone!"

"Of course! You knew I would before you ever came to the door," Joanne said laughing. She reached for the feathery black orphan.

Together, they went out in the yard and put the newcomer in with the Silkies. She settled in right away. They guessed the little hen was an Araucana because she laid coloured eggs.

Not too long after the little hen's arrival, the Seablooms were awakened by loud noises from the yard. Something was wrong!

"I'll go check, Ken," she whispered, as she dressed, then headed out the front door, giving Henry a pat on the way down the steps.

It was light enough to see white feathers scattered in the horse pasture. Nothing more remained of her little hens. The best guess was that one or more coyotes had a great feast.

"Odd," she thought, "Henry hasn't moved."

She patted him as she walked up onto the porch and noticed the little black hen nestled against his side. Henry was obviously protecting her.

The same morning after Joanne finished feeding her animals, she noticed Blackie was pecking around in the front yard and Henry still had not moved from the porch.

She went to him and unhooked his collar.

"Okay, boy, now you're free," she ruffled his head as a friendly release.

Henry looked quite content and wagged his tail but still, he did not move.

Joanne was beginning to worry. Obviously, something was wrong. This was not normal behavior for Henry! She stood, looking down at him, wondering what to do.

Then, very cautiously, he got up. On the porch where Henry had been was one of Blackie's pretty blue eggs!

Each day after that the Seablooms found an egg on the porch or in Henry's doghouse. They decided that Blackie was rewarding Henry with gifts for protecting her.

The dampness living near the coast was beginning to affect both the Shetland pony and Henry. They were slow and stiff.

"They aren't the only ones, Ken," Joanne grimaced. "Ten years in this climate is doing us no good!"

Ken looked at her in silent contemplation. When he spoke, it changed their lives forever.

"How would you like to find a new place; maybe the sunshine coast? It would be nearer to your folks."

Before she had a chance to respond, he gave her a big grin, "Yes, Joanne, animals and all!"

There was a brief moment of silent deliberation. Then came her resounding "Sure! Let's go for it! We could use more space anyway. I am sure the boys would be okay with it."

After that short conversation, every time Joanne picked up the paper, she opened the advertising section to Property for Sale. The little house in Mission was on the market and the search for a new home began.

The boys were delighted. It was exciting to go with their parents, looking for just the right house and some acreage. They had a big stake in this too. This was a great adventure.

One of their first excursions looking for a new home was a

journey to the Sunshine Coast. They stopped for a quick visit with Joanne's family.

"I am so disappointed. The houses here are way too expensive. We are going to have to look somewhere else, Mum," Joanne sighed.

"Since you are already here, why don't we take the boys over to the fair for a while," her Mum suggested.

"I had forgotten about the fair in Gibsons. I guess we had other things on our minds today. With the extra traffic, it did take us a bit longer to get through town." Joanne grinned to her Mum.

"Let's go! Ken encouraged. "The boys would get a kick out of it. At least the fair would be a positive note in an otherwise rather disappointing day."

They hadn't been at the fair very long when Ken came rushing back to Joanne from one of the booths. He grabbed her arm and pulled her in the direction of a photography display.

"There are pictures of Henry!" he announced.

Joanne gave him a solid skeptical glance and followed him across the fair grounds. Newfoundlands could look a bit like him, but why in the world would there be photos of him, especially here in Gibsons?

They stood and stared at the greeting cards for sale. There was absolutely no mistake. That was Henry's face!

"Is that your dog?" Ken and Joanne asked, almost simultaneously.

The young woman looked at them and then back at the Newfoundland on the cover of the card.

"He used to be," she said sadly.

"He was with me for a while. Unfortunately, I couldn't keep him."

"What did you call him?" Joanne asked.

"It was Henry," she said, "He was already named. You see, he was with me temporarily until they found a family that wanted to take him."

What followed was a conversation of shared memories.

The Seablooms and the photographer exchanged stories about the Newfoundland on the greeting card.

She was so happy to know where he was and to learn that he was finally a happy dog.

To this day, Henry's face can still be seen on greeting cards along the Sunshine Coast.

There were some disappointing months. No one seemed to want to buy the little house in Mission. Finding the right place was impossible! Every piece of property they liked cost too much money.

Then one day in the spring of 1991, things began to fall into place. They had a buyer for their little home with its one acre of land. Shortly after that, Joanne's Mum called. "Joanne, look in today's paper. There is an ad for a ten-acre hobby farm in Lone Butte. It sounds like just what you are looking for."

"Lone Butte? That's so far away!" Joanne listened as her mother read the information about the land.

Her mother's words convinced her they should at least have a look.

A very helpful realtor searched for information about schools and bus stops in the area. It sounded good. The next weekend, a neighbor agreed to take care of the animals and the Seablooms went on a "camping trip."

It was May and spring was just starting. There were buds on the trees and bushes. Occasional patches of snow lingered in shady places.

They took a look at the property and spent the night in a

nearby town called One Hundred Mile House. The next morning they decided to go back and have another look.

"You know," Ken said as they evaluated the ten acres, "This property meets all of our needs, except for fences."

"Ken, it also doesn't have a barn!" Joanne stated, as though he hadn't noticed.

"No problem," he assured. "You know we can fix that."

He turned to Joanne with a big grin on his face.

"Let's do it!" He urged, with an air of excitement in his voice. "It is perfect!"

"I would love to live here." Joanne echoed her husband's enthusiasm. "All of our critters would be happy here."

They made an offer and it was accepted.

The day after school was out for the summer, the Seabloom family, AKA the Clampets, prepared to move one Arabian horse, three Miniature horses, one Shetland pony, Henry, Maxzi and two other dogs, five cats, one potbellied pig, one chicken, four pigeons, two cockatiels, six huge turtles, three Jersey Wooly rabbits and three French Angora rabbits.

Transporting Henry and his family to the cariboo (dry backcountry) of British Columbia took some planning and a few volunteers. Seablooms had a minivan and their truck. They rented the largest moving van available as well as a small trailer. Joanne's parents brought their camper and transported Henry along with a full load of household belongings. A friend loaned them a brand new horse trailer and volunteered to haul it. Other friends and family signed on as helpers. They traveled in caravan on the record hottest day in twenty-five years. When they stopped for a meal at Cache Creek, Henry got a sponge-down with cool water. A trip that usually takes four-and-a-half-hours took nearly seven.

It was June 26, 1991 when the Seablooms, Henry and all, arrived on Fawn Creek Road, in Lone Butte, British Columbia.

CHAPTER NINE

Life in Lone Butte

The Seablooms, followed by a caravan of family and friends, turned into the driveway of their new home. The clear air was dry and wonderful to breathe.

Henry smiled his approval as his feet touched down on his new territory.

He had enjoyed the trip. After all, he had been a traveling man for more than half of his life.

Joanne put a bright yellow T-shirt on him and suggested, "Okay boys, take Henry for a long walk down the road. I want to make sure our neighbors know he is not a bear."

In his new home, Henry was content on his slider where he watched the settling-in process. Ken connected the slider to a clothesline at the back door. Now Henry could go up the stairs and into the kitchen as well as wander behind the back of the house.

A friend had helped Ken "Henry-proof" the fence around two acres, including the house, before they moved. The rest of the summer Ken spent pounding posts to enclose the entire ten acres. The boys and Joanne helped by dragging posts and wires to where supplies were needed. Dirk drove his motor bike from the work site to the house to get cold drinks for everybody. Henry was close by as they worked and the whole family kept careful watch and gave an occasional reminder if he wandered too far.

Crown land bordered their mini-ranch on two sides. There was also wilderness land close to their property. The combination of these wild areas provided space for free-roaming range cattle. It didn't take long for the newcomers to realize they needed good sturdy gates to keep the cattle out of their yard.

Fawn Lake was nearby for swimming. But her Newf was eleven and a half! Joanne wouldn't let him swim because he always got so excited; she was afraid he would have a heart attack.

Henry enjoyed his newfound freedom. But, for his own safety, he still spent the nights on his slider.

One evening not long after they moved in, Ken pointed out the window, "Look Joanne, there's a man on horseback coming down our driveway." They met him with a friendly greeting.

"Hi, my name's Pete," he smiled and from horseback he reached down and shook hands with Ken. "My wife, Sharon, and I live about three kilometers down the road. Guess you could call us neighbours. We want to welcome your family and your 'bear' to the area. Also, I want to let you know those cows wandering on the road aren't mine!"

The visit was short but set the basis for a lasting friendship. They all laughed, thanked Pete for coming and waved him a friendly goodbye.

With warm feelings of acceptance, Ken and Joanne began another day of unpacking, filling cupboards and closets, and establishing order in their new world.

Since the fencing was secure around the house, Henry spent less time on his slider. He showed little desire to leave home unless someone left the gate open. Just a verbal reminder could discourage his departure. He liked Lone Butte as much as they did!

When Joanne was outside, Henry was always with her. He enjoyed mingling with the other animals, especially Buddy Boy.

Henry never got in the way when she was moving horses to pasture. He was smart and careful.

One hot summer day the phone rang. "Hi, this is Pete. Three of our cows broke down our fence and are headed your way. I thought you might keep an eye out for them."

"I don't see them, Pete, but I'll watch for them," Joanne assured him.

"Thanks a lot. I don't want them to get in with the range cows, and I figure they are going to show up at your place pretty soon."

"We aren't too used to cows but if we see them, we'll try to get them into our pasture," Joanne chuckled. "I'll get Ken to help."

Seablooms went down to their gate. The timing was perfect! Here came Pete's cows; there was no mistaking them for all three were wearing halters.

As Ken swung open the gate, they debated how best to get three stray cows off the road. Just then Henry joined the team.

The Newfoundland went out through the gate and headed straight for the cattle. He moved behind them and confidently herded them into the yard and on into the pasture before the unbelieving eyes of his family.

Three days later, Pete rode his horse down to take his errant bovines home. They discussed how to get the cattle out of the pasture, down the driveway, and through the gate. Henry stood there, wagging his tail. He seemed so eager to have a part in the event.

"Let's see if Henry can be of any help," Joanne suggested, as she opened the pasture gate.

Henry rushed in and herded the cows out of the pasture, down the driveway, and through the front gate. He was definitely in charge as he sent them in the right direction toward home. Pete's face registered shock and surprise as he witnessed the herding demonstration.

"Hey, this is great! He can just take them all the way home for me," Pete grinned.

"No, no, Pete. It's too hot to let him herd them all the way to your place," Joanne said with a smile, "He is eleven, that's pretty old for this kind of work."

Ken turned toward the house. "I'll get the truck. We'll give him a few minutes to enjoy herding cattle then we'll pick him up down the road."

"Good idea! I don't want him over-doing it," she said with a big grin on her face.

She watched him with great wonder and pride. Then she whispered softly, "Henry, you really are something special."

One evening long after the summer had turned to fall, Ken and Joanne sat in their living room. The sun splashed across the black furry rug-like shape on the floor, which snored softly.

Ken nodded to his wife as he reflected on the big dog's behaviors, "Henry is one smart dog. I don't think I have ever witnessed anything that was any more fun than watching him herd those cattle. That was fantastic!"

Joanne nodded her head in agreement. She looked at her treasured Newfoundland. It was peaceful, somehow, when he liked to be in the house with them. It was never for very long. Just a short nap, and he was at the door asking to go out again.

As the year went by, Henry increased his time in the house. Was it because he was older? Maybe not as able to handle the cold? Or, perhaps it was just that he enjoyed being near his family? Joanne wondered.

"You know, Ken, Henry is twelve. I think we ought to consider getting another Newfoundland." Joanne offered. "We can't expect to have him much longer. I don't want to be without a Newf again!"

"Yea, I guess you're right." Ken agreed. "Where do we start? You've looked off and on ever since we got Henry and there's never been another one available."

"This time, I am going to look up some breeders. I really want a puppy." She reached down and rubbed Henry's head and neck. "It's time, isn't it, old dear."

Ken watched his wife, the ultimate animal lover. "She wants another animal? Haven't we got enough?" he thought.

Secretly, Ken knew his opinion didn't change things a lot when Joanne wanted to add to the collection. "Why not?" was his confirmation.

The next day, Joanne began her research for the right puppy. They agreed to get a Newfoundland that they could show and breed. Temperament and longevity were primary factors in the search. It was not an easy task. But when the day finally came, and he heard her confident announcement, he understood.

"I've found one, Ken. We need to go look at her." Hesitantly she mentioned that it was about an eight-hour drive each way.

"Are you serious?" Ken exclaimed, thinking about the destination. "That includes a ferry ride too, right?"

After a brief moment of contemplation then he gave her a big grin, "Why not!"

"You are a good judge of animals and people," She bragged to him. "This time we are buying a puppy. That is a lot different from taking in a rescue Newfoundland."

Joanne called the breeder and arranged a visit. Then she talked with a neighbour who agreed to care for their animals while the family was away.

"The breeder said we could see her parents and her grand parents. I'm really glad of that." Joanne confided. The conversation between them drifted into dreamy planning of her future which included much more than just being a playmate for Henry.

"This is Annie," the breeder said as he let her out of her pen. Joanne was disappointed. The puppy looked just like a black Irish setter. It jumped up on her and licked her face, and wiggled about them with boundless energy.

"Is this really going to be a beautiful Newfoundland?" she wondered. Then tactfully confronted the breeder with her concerns.

He laughed. "She will be a beauty," he assured them. "Lots of Newfoundlands look pretty gangly at this age. She'll grow out of it."

He took them on a short tour of the kennel so they could see the relatives. They saw Annie's parents, and grand-parents and met a very impressive Newf named Rastus. This was a confidence builder for Ken and Joanne. Based on their observations they came to believe that she would indeed turn out to be a beautiful Newf. She was sweet-natured and lively and they decided that she was truly the right pup for them.

During the journey home the Seablooms discussed names but made no definite decisions. It was 2:00 A.M. when they arrived at Lone Butte. They decided to let the pup sleep that night in the truck with food, water and chew toys.

Early the next morning she met Henry and the crew at Lone Butte. She was bouncy and active, perfectly suited to farm life.

On the pup's first day home with the Seablooms the breeder called to say he was ready to send in the registration papers. He needed a name. That day, Annie became Katie.

In his early years Henry occasionally had tested his freedom and tried to sneak off to the neighbours nearby. After Katie came into his life he never tried again. There was instant bonding between the old dog and the pup. Henry began to act like a puppy again. He played with her and taught her to retrieve a toy. He taught her to relieve herself in the trees and not on the lawn. The young female was bright and learned fast. This was just as the Seablooms hoped it would be for Henry had much to teach.

Henry actually taught her too well. She learned the boundaries of their perimeter fence, she learned not to go near the front gate. As a beautiful adult, Katie watched. If Henry moved too close to the front gate, Katie began her tattle-tale bark and came running to tell Joanne.

All Katie needed was her happy life on the farm where she had space to run off her super energy and interact with the farm animals. Plans in the future were to breed her if she was free of hip dysplasia. They hoped for an OFA (Orthopedic Foundation for Animals) certification and eventually a puppy from Katie. Soon Henry would be gone and they wanted the company of other Newfoundlands.

Long before it was time to breed Katie, Joanne began to research pedigrees for good bloodlines. She remembered the beautiful dog named Rastus. When she made the call, she learned that Katie's breeder had died and Rastus was in a new home in Mission.

In response to Joanne's inquiry, the conversation was cordial and Rastus' new owner was eager to cooperate.

"He is thirty-six inches tall," Joanne was told enthusiastically. "He is OFA certified and a Champion."

"We have plenty of time," Joanne reminded Rastus' owner. "We will keep in touch."

Months later, Rastus' owner called to say many things had changed. They needed to place him in a good home and offered him to the Seablooms.

Ken, "We saw that dog, and I don't believe he is as tall as she said. His pedigree is great. I really didn't pay that much attention to him."

"It's a lot closer to drive to Mission, Joanne. Is that what you really want to do?"

"They said we could make payments for him, Ken" Joanne considered, "His bloodline is a pretty good match. The only way we will really know is if we go see him again."

Joanne made a quick call about the dog named Rastus. She made arrangements with the owner to go for a visit on the weekend.

Back to old familiar territory, the Seablooms drove to Mission to meet Rastus.

It was love at first sight, even if he greeted them with slobber flying.

"He's big, Ken, but he's not thirty-six inches. I'll bet he is thirty-two," Joanne guessed. She had her hands on his head, feeling his back, sides, and bone structure.

"What a sweetie!" Joanne sighed to the owner, as she reached out to him and gave him a big hug.

"You say he has always lived in the kennel? He's three and a half! Hmmm."

Both Ken and Joanne were impressed with the big tail-wagging creature. There was something about him that made Joanne feel sad. " . . . his whole life as a kennel dog," she thought.

His eyes met hers in a long uninterrupted study. They were dark brown and it seemed to her that they looked straight into her heart. She could almost read a sense of longing in his expression.

"Rastus is very insecure," the owner spoke, breaking the encounter, "he will need a kennel to sleep in."

She gestured to the small trailer that was currently his sleeping quarters.

70

Ken looked at it for a moment and turned to Joanne, "We'll figure out something." The Seablooms worked out an agreement with the owner and left a deposit. They made plans to come back for him in two weeks, after they made arrangements for him at home.

Like Henry, he traveled in their truck covered by a canopy. But when he arrived at Lone Butte, he was not anxious to leave the security of his travel quarters. This was just as the previous owner had warned.

Ken made a ramp for him to walk down but he refused. He lay quietly against the far end of the truck.

Henry and Katie happily wagged their tails and did their part as a great welcoming committee. Still, Rastus didn't move.

Ken and Joanne decided to let him come out on his own, so they left the tailgate open and watched from the house.

After a time, Henry leaped into the truck and licked Rastus as if to say, "You can come out, you are home." And before long he leaped out of the truck with Rastus right behind. Neither one used the ramp.

Katie greeted Rastus and the three Newfoundlands acted as if they had been friends all of their lives. There would never be a squabble between them.

The big Newfoundland with a sad soul began a new life in Lone Butte. It took a long time for his personality to shine through. Once he adjusted to his new environment, he relaxed and developed into a big loveable teddy bear. Rastus never slept in the private space Ken provided for him. Instead, he chose to sleep in the garden under Seablooms' bedroom window. To this day they can hear him snoring peacefully in his chosen quarters.

Katie and Henry remained a team as they interacted with the other animals on the farm. One winter, the Seablooms had a young Miniature horse colt, Little Archie, that was extremely ill. Katie and Henry were constantly attentive to the sick colt. Joanne had old Henry dressed in a Miniature Horse blanket to protect him from the cold. She put Henry's coat on Little Archie and made Henry sleep in the house that night. He gave her a few "looks" but accepted what he could not change.

As Henry grew older, they often took him along during the winter when they went to Lone Butte to their tack shop. They didn't want to leave him at home outside in the cold. It wasn't long until Henry developed quite a fan club of friends in Lone Butte who came and went from the shop.

Each time the farrier came to the farm to trim horses hooves, Henry knew there would be special treats. As the trimmed hoof pieces fell to the ground, he was there to grab a tasty morsel and find a place nearby to munch happily on his prize. When he could no longer get around well the delicacies were delivered to him at the house!

As Henry got older, Katie attentively watched over him. Joanne helped Henry out to the front yard one day when he was not very mobile. He liked to spend time with Katie and Rastus. Katie had been chewing on her favorite bone. When Henry joined them, Katie made a special effort to bring her bone to Henry. After awhile, she took it from Henry and gave it to Rastus. When it was her turn, she carefully took the bone out of Rastus' mouth and chewed it. When she decided it was Henry's turn again, she placed the bone right between his paws.

Ken brought home a computer in 1988 to keep inventory for their tack shop where they sold horse and dog supplies. They went on the Internet in 1996. But it was not until 1997 that Joanne showed real interest.

One day she found a web site for Newfoundland Dogs. She entered some basic information as requested and included information about her Newfs.

Things got interesting in a hurry.

She had requests for more stories about her dogs. People were especially interested in hearing more about her old Newfoundland.

One morning in February of 1997 she got up and turned on her computer.

"Ken! I just checked my e-mail. I have 70 messages!"

PART TWO

HENRY

Humankind has not woven the web of life.
We are but one thread within it.
Whatever we do to the web, we do to ourselves.
All things are bound together.
All things connect.

Chief Seattle

Art work compliments of Geraldine Welburn,
Joanne Seabloom's Mother

A WHOLE NEW WORLD

A Letter from Joanne to Claire　　　February 6, 1998

A whole new world opened up for me once we got Internet. The day we got it I was trying to see what the net was all about. I decided to look up Newfoundland Dogs. At the time we had Henry, Katie and Rastus. Well, I found a site on Newfoundlands. It asked for my e-mail address as well as my name and address. I didn't really know that I was signing onto a list at the time. Was I ever excited to see e-mail coming in! The welcome letter said to introduce my Newfs and myself. So, I did. I told the ages and names of my Newfs. Well, before I knew it there were letters coming in from all over the world asking me to tell more about Henry, as they had never heard of a Newf so old. This had never occurred to me. I frequently had people asking about Henry, so I started sending the odd note to the list. One day a thread (an e-mail conversation theme) was started on rescue Newfs. So, I sent in Henry's story. I was overwhelmed by the response! But, it seemed that many people grew to really love a Newf they had never met. Once Henry became ill, I was very upset but tried to make his progress as cheerful as I could. I discovered that keeping my spirits up meant keeping Henry's spirits up.

Sunday, November 9, 1997
Joanne's first words to the Newf-List

We were lost without a Newf after losing our beloved Duchess. We tried putting our names in with many all breed clubs and pet rescue groups. In fact, we were volunteers for the local SPCA (Society for the Prevention to Animals) as there was no shelter in Mission where we lived. We wanted a Newf so badly; it was like a big void in our lives. But, we never got a call.

I constantly scanned the newspapers. I spoke to breeders. But, at the time we just couldn't afford a puppy.

One day, we were in North Vancouver visiting Ken's Mum. We were just about to leave when I saw the ad for Pets Unlimited. Among the list of pets needing adoption, there was a Newfoundland listed. I couldn't wait! I started dialing, but couldn't get through. So, on the way home, we stopped at phone booths along the way. I finally got through right at a busy intersection and could barely hear the lady! Looking back, I guess it seems kind of silly not to wait until we got home. But, I thought that possibly this dog would be in the Vancouver area and we didn't want to wait one extra minute!

I was told to call the next day for details on the dog that the woman said was still available. I then learned that Henry had been looking for a home for two years! I still can't understand why we never heard about him sooner! He was on the Sechelt Peninsula, so we had to wait until the following weekend to go and see him. This entailed a trip by ferry and could be combined with a visit to my parents who lived near Gibsons. Our sons were small, so of course we had to be sure that Henry would like them. There was no doubt in our minds. (When we made the journey) We were on our way to pick up our dog!

Joanne Seabloom

Part Two

To our readers   **September 25, 1998**

Newf-List readers wanted to have Henry entered in the "Oldest Living Newfoundland" contest. It was sponsored by Claire Carr and her daughter, JoAnn Wucherer as a personal tribute to old Newfs from 1993 through 1997. Members of the Newfoundland Club of America were eligible to enter their American Kennel Club registered dogs. Beginning in 1998 the Newfoundland Club of America assumed responsibility for the award.

To Claire   **Henry was 17yrs 20days**

" . . . That is really interesting about the Oldest Newf Award! That was a really good idea! I certainly understand that the oldest Newf has to be a member (AKC Reg. and NCA). We have the greatest award of all! Henry in person! Yes, he is certainly loved!"

Can you believe that the beginning of September the vet arrived to put him to sleep as we thought he was dying. I was just devastated, but didn't want him suffering. Imagine my amazement and relief when after a thorough examination, we found out that he would recover! That vet appointment was September 6th, just three months before his seventeenth birthday! We feel very fortunate to have Henry, especially without pain. Well, he is a little stiff.

I know that Henry's time will come, but until then, we will enjoy him every day that we can! Have a great day!

Joanne Seabloom
C-21 Fawn Creek Road
RR#1. Lone Butte,
B.C., Canada VOK1XO

Henry was 16 yrs 11 mo 17days

To Newf-List, November 23, 1997

Hi There,

I've been getting a lot of inquiries about Henry. He seems to be getting very popular! I'm having a hard time keeping up with all his e-mail! He will be 17 years old on December 6, 1997. Henry is doing pretty well. His heart murmur doesn't seem to be a problem and he has adapted well to having just a little sight in one eye. His hearing is excellent and he still has his good humour! I no longer have to hang on to his T-shirt all the time. He can be let out to go for a short walk on his own. Katie always guides him now. I always am sure to take him for a good walk at least twice a day. Henry on my right side, Katie on my left with Rastus right behind and often Buddy Boy behind him. Buddy boy is a Shetland pony almost 51 years old.

Henry is not quite as demanding as he was. He was constantly taking advantage of me and howling for attention. He knows exactly when the computer is turned on! As I said, very good hearing! He doesn't seem to be having the headaches recently. He still calls me, but because he wants a cuddle!

It is funny how Henry likes to go and visit his old pal, Buddy Boy. They are both almost blind. I used to be worried that Buddy would step on Henry. Katie watched carefully and worried too! But, Henry just lies down near him with his nose up. Buddy shuffles his feet until he gets very close and they can touch noses. It is cute to see. In the warm weather, the three Newfs and Buddy Boy would lie by the front door together. Now that we have snow, Henry just likes to go out for about ten or so quick visits per day.

Well, that's all the current news of Henry! Have a great day!

Joanne, Henry, Katie, Rastus

Hi Claire,   **Henry was 16yrs 11mo 20days**

Here is a story for you. I met Carol (not in person) on the list when she joined. She had a Newf named Piper. One day an e-mail came to Henry from Piper. We had so much fun between Henry and Piper writing and sending virtual greetings. Henry loved for me to turn on the computer and I always read him the letters. It was something he really enjoyed.

Well, have a great day! Joanne

To the Newf-List   **Henry was 16yrs 11mo 28days**

Hi All,

As most of you know, Henry's 17th Birthday is on Saturday, December sixth. He seems to know, with that dignified expression of his. As none of the "listers" (those who communicate by way of e-mail to the Newf-List) live nearby his Birthday party will probably be just with his family.

Henry is doing pretty well. Although his sight is getting poor, he gets around alright. He rarely has headaches and dizzy spells are fewer. He is a bit slow getting up and takes his time backing up to lie down. But when I go outside with Henry for a walk, there is a spring in his step! He is still a cheerful fellow and can always make me smile.

If I leave Henry's side for just a minute when we are outdoors, he makes a beeline for the front door. If I'm a bit delayed, Rastus and Katie lie on either side of him keeping him warm. If it's cold out, Katie runs to grab my hand and Rastus stays with Henry. It is funny, if Rastus and Katie don't notice Henry by the door at first, then he does his woo-wooing! They go to him running! By the time I get there, you should see the looks! Well, I have to apologize profusely!

83

Many of you asked me to nominate Henry for the Oldest Newf Contest. I believe Henry doesn't qualify as he was born and raised in Canada. I think that the contest is for the AKC dogs only. Thank you all for thinking of him, though. Well, have a great day!

                    Joanne, Henry, Katie, Rastus

                                    Henry was 17yrs 3 days
To Newf-List from Joanne-Birthday Party!
Hi All,

I want to thank you for the wonderful greetings for Henry's 17th birthday! There were over 400 messages for him! These included personal messages, virtual gifts, flowers, cards, hugs, and food of everything from caviar and champagne to birthday cakes and biscuits! We had a lot of fun with them. It was great receiving the homemade cards and photos of many of Henry's online pals!

Henry had a quiet party with his friends and family here. He got a nice new bright red shirt. He had special stew and then cookies and had a nap. Then his friends from across the road came over with bacon jerky treats and a big box of senior dog biscuits. Then he had another snooze. Henry asked to go outside about ten times during the day. He expects a treat every time he comes in. The next day, he kept whining. Every time I checked to see what was wrong, he started to howl. He can sound quite mournful! Well, there was nothing wrong with him. He just wanted more goodies and birthday stew! So, now we have a very spoiled old fellow! But, of course, he has earned it!

Today he is feeling pretty neglected. Gord, the vet, came to see Zarmid and not him! Zar is an Arabian stallion who is also getting old. So, I guess I'd better go take Henry for a walk so he can see his pals. I tried to send a thank you to everyone who sent Henry a birthday greeting. Some bounced back and I got a bit confused. I hope I didn't miss anyone.

Henry has had a full 17 years and I hope we have him a few more yet! He is happy and feeling pretty good which is the main thing. Have a great day!

Joanne, Henry, Katie, Rastus - of "Geriatric Park"

To the Newf-List   **Henry was 17yrs 1mo 17days**

Hi There,

Well, as most of you know, Henry was 17 years old Dec 6, 1997. He has been a healthy dog until he developed Canine Geriatric Vestibular Disease (CGVD) last summer. I'm sure he pulled through with all the encouragement, prayers, and good wishes from all of you list members!

We had a lot of fun with Henry and his cyber-girlfriend. We exchanged a lot of fun messages, until she passed away last month from Cushings Disease. Henry always started to whine when the computer was turned on. I read him all his messages. I think he really enjoyed it. It was very hard to lose Piper, though we never actually met in person. It is funny, after Piper passed away, he has never whined at the sound of the computer.

Henry had me up with him to let him out several times during the nights, but had been doing pretty well, despite having gone blind. Carol sent us a book, The Lighthouse Dog in memory of Piper. I read him the book and told him about the pictures. He

85

relaxed and sighed and slept right through the night! We both love the book. So, now I read more often to Henry. He seems to enjoy his walks through the snow, so I keep the lawn shoveled for him. He gets that determined look and he is off, nose to the ground. He is still happy and loves his hugs and massages. He no longer likes to be brushed, so he just gets a little done at a time. I think I would shave him if it weren't so cold outside. His coat is shiny and soft and his eyes still reflect good humor.

He has the odd time that he gets a bit disoriented when he is coming back to the front door. But, though his walk is a bit stilted, he has had quite a lot of strength, especially when he wants to go in a different direction then I do!

I have noticed that recently, Henry's old pal, Buddy Boy, is often waiting by the front door for him to come out in the morning. Buddy gets fed at the back door. He shuffles over to Henry and they touch noses before he goes around back to wait for his breakfast. Buddy is almost blind. (We call it selective blindness) but he never steps on Henry. We had a white truck and he kept bumping in to it. We traded it for a darker colour. Since then he has no problems.

Since I started this I have seen a difference in Henry. He seems to be having a bout of vertigo. He was happily gnawing on his bone and then threw up. He can't stand and had to be lifted. This is what he went through before. We will see how he is tomorrow. Last time, he was unable to walk for a few days. It took him three weeks for the vertigo to stop. I know we can't expect to have Henry too much longer, but as he isn't in pain, we will enjoy him as long as we can.

Well, that's all the news of Henry. Sorry this is so long.

Joanne

A Gift for Sarah

"Please love me, don't leave me," those eyes seemed to say,
When you offered a home to Sarah that day.
"My family can't keep me, I've problems galore,
I have fits, I am clumsy and lots of things more.
I can't help what I am. Please love me, don't leave me,
I'll fit in with your life, just wait and you'll see."

So home Sarah came, our dreams had come true,
A Newf for our family – the dogs welcomed her too.
Very soon it appeared that she'd settled right in,
Showed her pleasure at life with that typical grin,
Saved the kids from the drowning that threatened each night,
When mom bathed them – well, to a Newf's mind they might!

A month she's been with you, or a little bit less,
Your life has now changed in ways you'd not guess.
A Newf in the house is a gift and a boon,
You'd just never have thought it would happen so soon.

But now she is sick and your're worried and sad,
You knew it might happen, but not quite this bad.
Her eyes pled for that help a dog's family can give,
"Please love me, don't leave me, I've life I must live.
I've your family to raise, to protect and to love,
You came into my life like a gift from above."

"Please hold me and hug me, be patient and kind,
I need you, don't leave me. I'm sure you won't mind
Giving me all your love in your hearts you can find."
You silently cry when she leaves you each time,
Your heart breaks a bit more, there's no reason or rhyme.
Except she's a Newf and a special one too,
She came into your lives and your dreams all came true.

"Please love us, don't leave us, we need you, you cry.
If it made you feel better we'd make pink pigs fly!
As it is, you don't need that, thank heavens above.
But instead we can offer unconditional love."

The world prays for Sarah, a Newf who's in need.
If love helps to cure her, she's lucky indeed.
We're all there for you, Sarah, to help you pull through.
And Billee, please know that you're in our thoughts too.

    Liz Bradbury and the Scotish Gang
    Toby-Newf, Annie, Belle and Jaz the Bernese and the
    6 Feline Friends
    SCOTLAND

Hi Claire,   **Henry was 17yrs 1mo 18days**

    I was writing an update for the list. Before I got finished, he became ill. I was up all night with Him. He cannot walk. Yesterday he was feeling much better and was eating well. He has slept a lot and our neighbor, Kirk, has been over several times to lift him in and out for me. Last night he slept through until 6:30 A.M., which was a nice change. I felt it was a little early to call

Kirk so I managed to get him out on my own. Of course, Ken had already gone to work! Henry is improved. He tried to walk a few steps with me supporting him with his T-shirt. Getting him in was really tough! Of course, both my boys were sound asleep! I got a quilted horse blanket he sleeps on and rolled him onto it. I dragged him back to the door. He got the idea and relaxed, letting me pull him over the ice! We struggled up the step into the house and he had a good breakfast. I bet he has a good snooze! He loves lying in the snow. I just don't want him to get chilled. I know he is living on borrowed time, but it would be nice to have him just a little longer.

Joanne

To our readers   **November 10, 1999**

After Henry went to live with Seablooms, Joanne began an extensive phone search to verify his date of birth. She contacted his first family, the attending veterinarian, one of his past foster homes as well as his last foster family. The responses were the same. Henry was born on December 6, 1980. By one woman, she was told that all of her calls wouldn't make him any younger!

Hi Claire,   **Henry was 17yrs, 2 mo 1 day**

The CKC records are so incomplete.

Well, I have to run. Henry (AKA Angelface) is calling. Very demanding! Have a good day!

Joanne, Henry, Katie, Rastus

A thread began on the Newf-List regarding Henry as a mascot.

I'd like to put a proposal before the group. Why don't we all vote in HENRY as the official Newf-L Mascot?

What a delightfully wonderful idea! I count sixty four paws and hands up in this house! (Okay, so I counted back feet too, and all the cats who were VERY resistant to the idea.)
Pamela van Giessen, Zillah, Allegra and Company
Illinois   USA

As far as the Henry as Mascot question? Count me IN. What a guy! I already have Henry photos as my wallpaper on the opening screen. It is much more attractive than the Windows clouds. What a handsome hound!!!!!!!
A friend in
Oklahoma   USA

Other voices from friends:
Yes, Woo-Woo, Wooof, Wuf, Arf and Roarf
AYE

Henry has become an icon to all Newf people throughout the entire world. I will always remember him as our mascot for the Newf-L.
Greg and Mary DeRosa and Kona
New Jersey   USA

Hi Claire, **Henry was 17yrs, 2mo 18days**

Henry is doing pretty well. He had me up five or six times last night. He had to go but didn't want to go outside when I opened the door. Then he wanted a drink of water. Then he wet his bed and wanted it changed. Now! Then another drink. Then a snack. (I slipped in an aspirin hoping it would get him to sleep.) Then at 4:00 A.M. he wanted to go out. I had to wait a half-hour after I lugged him out to do his business. He goes lying down and I have to move him immediately or I hear about it! Of course, I was hoping to keep him quiet so he didn't keep everyone else awake! Finally he was ready to come in. I rubbed his ears and fed him breakfast and he has slept ever since. I am tired and have swollen glands and a cough, so I could use a break. Oh well, he is feeling good. It is a beautiful sunny day. If it wasn't so icy out, it would be a great day to play with the dogs and horses! It is melting fast but it freezes at night.

Pat Escalante is hostess of the Newfdog chat. I usually go to that on Wednesday evenings. She e-mailed me to say that she had made a web page for Henry. She used his story I sent to the list. There are pictures on it. Just look until you see the picture of me with my Newfs. Click on Henry. Have a great day!

Joanne

Email to Claire from Joanne about Piper, Henry's cyber girlfriend

I really got into Henry stories after making friends with Carol Batchelder online. At the time she had 13 Newfs, most elderly and/or invalids. Her Piper was Henry's cyber girlfriend. She passed away before Henry. We had a lot of fun with Henry and Piper writing to each other. It was silly, but fun. Henry used to lie in the kitchen and listen for the computer to be turned on. I would read him his letters. When he could no longer get up the stairs he would perk his head up if the computer turned on. But when Piper passed away I was upset and he just seemed to know. Carol sent him the child's book, The Lighthouse Dog. My family made fun of me as I sat and read it to him several times. He just loved it. One day, I turned and saw Ken video taping me reading to Henry. Ha Ha!

Joanne

Hi Claire,   **Henry was 17yrs 3mo**

Henry would be honoured to have his picture on the cover of the Oldest Living Newfoundland 1997 binder that you are taking to the National Specialty. Thanks.

The e-mail got to be a bit much! I can delete the Newf-stuff but I have made friends and would probably accidentally delete personal messages too! Henry gets a lot of e-mail. Even one lister has a Hedgehog named "Henry Hedgie" after him! Goodnight!

Joanne

Hi Claire,   **Henry was 17yrs 3mo 17days**

Henry has been very time consuming! He has discovered that he can walk now that the ice is gone. He has gotten his confidence back and is walking pretty well. I have to steady him but no longer half carry him. I felt sure that if I cared for him as an invalid over the winter, that he would walk again. He is very

92

demanding. Today it has been raining and he no longer likes to get wet. He used to love to lie out in the rain. The colder the better! Now he is very fussy. Katie rushed in to stand on his bedding and got her muddy footprints all over it. Henry can't see but he likes his bed spotless. He lets me know in no uncertain terms that his bedding has to be changed! I seem to be running up and down the flights of stairs all day and all night! Plus doing his laundry. But I'm glad to see him doing so well. If I could just get him back on a normal routine! He wants a drink, then a snack, then a look outside. I try to pull him out but he is very stubborn and plants his feet and digs right in! Then he whines! He does heavy breathing. Then he howls! I guess I have spoiled him a bit. He wants attention from about 3:30 P.M. until about 12:00 midnight. I just get to sleep and at 3:00 A.M. he wants to go out for a walk. Then I am up with him until about 5:00 A.M. Everyone else ignores him if I'm around. He hates it when I am on the computer. He heard it dial in. So, of course he is yelling at me right now. Poor guy, I guess he is bored. I will go and read to him for a few minutes. His hearing is excellent and he always knows exactly where I am and what I'm doing. Quite the character! I just can't get angry with him. But, I am getting awfully tired!

Katie is being a real pig and eating everything in sight! She appears wider through the ribs but hard to tell. She is a very active girl and real fit, but I think I feel a bit of a tummy! So keep your fingers crossed. Maybe she will have puppies.

I am still waiting for Cameo to have her foal.

Got to run and read Henry his book.

Joanne

Hi Joanne,   **Date unknown**

No matter how Henry's health seems to be fading you always have something positive to say about him. This makes me feel both happy that he is tramping along and terrified that he is packing his bags for the trip over the bridge. When Henry finally consents to leave you in the care of Katie and Rastus, I will mourn his passing like I would one of my own family members. You see, I do not look at April, my Newf, as being my dog. I look at her and see my flesh and blood, a part of my family, not a pet. From all you have written and shared, I feel like Henry is my long-lost uncle in the mountains. When he is gone the Earth will cry and the Heavens shudder. Me, I will shed tears with you.

Today he is with you and I know you spend every minute available simply sharing the time he has left being with his human.

God bless you both, and may Katie and Rastus live the same amazing life Henry is now enjoying. I must close now to find some tissue!

Keep on Newfin'
Sean Manson
Nova Scotia   CANADA

Hi Claire,   **Henry was 17yrs 4mo 18days**

I'm afraid I haven't had a lot of time to get to the Henry stuff. My poor old brain is a bit overtired.   Katie had her three puppies April 21, (1998). Since then I have been practically living with her in her whelping doghouse. Now, it seems I should have let her have her puppies in the barn. I am watching Sunshine closely and had to move out there now for the nights. So,

I have to make the rounds from barn to house to see Henry and walk him and then to Katie and puppies. Hmmm, I do have a family somewhere. Ken is dong the cooking.

Sunshine has lost her last two foals and I'm doing my darndest to have this one arrive living! We have our old camper attached to the barn and our old video camera set up so I can lie down in the camper and watch her on TV.

The puppies are adorable. I spend a lot of time with Katie and them. Poor Katie took a long time having them, but she is just fine. We are keeping a male and the female is going to a terrific home in Cranbrook with people on the Newf-List.

In answer to your question about my critters, I now have six Newfs, one Toy Poodle, one Siamese, one Manx, one fifty one year old Shetland pony, five Arabian horses, eight Miniature horses, two canaries, six turtles, three rabbits, two sons and one husband. A very patient husband, I might add! He puts up with me and all my critters. Well, got to run and take Sunshine's temperature and check puppies, etc. Henry is actually having a snooze, so it is peaceful! Rastus really needs a lot of attention these days Have a great day!

Joanne, Henry, Katie, Rastus

To the Newf-List   **Henry was 17yrs 4mo 20days**
Hi There.

Thought you would like to know Katie had three pups. One died. Henry is demanding a lot of attention these days. He can't see, but he is very interested in sniffing the air and knows all about those puppies! He likes to take his walks as close as he can get and then "accidentally" has to flop down nearby. Katie doesn't even mind. She actually comes and has a visit with him before he is up and off on his stroll.

Henry is not too mobile these days. I have to support him with a T-shirt, but I think he thinks he is! He seems very happy and likes to lounge on the lawn with Rastus if I take the time and pull up a chair. Well, Henry is calling for a snack! Must run. Have a great day!

Joanne, Henry, Katie, Rastus and pups

To the Newf-List   **Henry was 17yrs 5mo**
Hi There,

Henry is doing pretty well. He is almost seventeen and a half. He is happy and likes me to spend time with him. He loves to go for walks in the front yard. He just charges around with me gripping his T-shirt and holding him up. Henry can no longer walk without being supported as he travels with his nose to the ground. He thinks he gets around pretty well, until I lose my grip and he does a somersault. Poor guy. He never seems bothered by it. I guess because he gets fussed over a lot! He can stand just fine on his own and has a lot of strength. Boy, try steering him in the direction that he doesn't want to go! He has taken a great interest in the puppies. Katie is quite protective but in Henry's case it seemed that she wanted him to come near so he could smell them. Finally, he has been introduced to the puppies. He thought it was great until Katie left him baby sitting! He can no longer see but his nose works well. The nice thing is that Henry is not in pain. He is just getting a bit less mobile gradually. He is still our happy fellow. Hope you all have a great day!

Joanne, Henry, Katie, Rastus

Hi Claire.   **Henry was 17yrs 5mo 4days**

Things have been busy here! After I e-mailed you that there were 3 puppies, I went to check them and one was squashed under Katie. I had been away only one half-hour! She seemed confused about having three after the third one was born a day later than the first two. Then, at eight days of age, the female was down to bones and hypothermic. I practically lived in that whelping box! The vet checked her three times and it is good news, fortunately. The male is such a pig and pushes her away. She is very active and got chilled. So, I just completely bottle-fed her. She also had a navel infection which couldn't be seen but I could just tell. The vet asked me to take her elsewhere as he had no luck with failing puppies. Hmmmmm. I went in to get the antibiotics and had her heart checked. Of course he got paid for my diagnosis! She is now a roly-poly 3 pounds and her brother is about 6 pounds. I am living in the barn waiting for Sunshine's foal. I am hoping to save this one. So the puppy lived there with me too. It is very helpful to be able to watch Sunshine on the video monitor.

On May eighth she had a live foal! Hurrah! And a filly at last! This time I was there to pull it and it was even a normal birth! Her name is Seabloom Penny in My Pocket.

Still haven't named our puppy. He is going by the name of Kong. The female is Velcro, named by her family-to-be. Got to run and feed Velcro. Henry is finally asleep! Have a great day!

Joanne, Henry, Katie, Rastus and pups

Hi Claire,   8:08am –Henry was 17yrs 5 mo 20days

Our pup is five weeks old. We still can't agree on a call name yet. His registered name is Seabloom Nightwind Navigator (so far anyway).

Henry has had me up since 3:00 A.M. I guess since he is blind, he can't tell time anymore. He wants me to walk him. Finally, I get him out and he has done his business, so I give him water and a treat and crawl into bed. A few minutes later, he is howling again. So, I give him another rubdown and rub his ears and head, more water and give him an early breakfast with aspirin. Back to bed, but he is whining again! Back down those stairs and help him outside. Take him for another little walk. Then he plunks himself down and won't budge. Along come Katie and Rastus for hugs too. When Henry is good and ready, back we go to the house. I lug him in and give him water and cookie. Back to bed. About fifteen minutes later, he calls me again! Finally, I took him out and left him out. Came back to bed for 15 minutes until he started to howl. Brought him in again. By this time, it was 5:00 A.M. Finally got to sleep and then he started howling again. I just couldn't budge until 5:45 A.M. He had to go. Took him out and walked with him until he was ready to just plunk himself down. So, left him while I fed the horses early. Then brought him in for his breakfast and he is finally quiet! This has been his little routine lately. I'm finding that it is really tiring. But he looks rather cheerful about the whole thing.

Well. gotta run. Have a great day!

Joanne

Hi Claire,   **9:15pm – Henry was 17 yrs 5mo 20days**

Today Henry fell down the stairs. I felt so bad. I couldn't get to him to keep him from falling. He is fine though. Dirk and I carried him upstairs and then I took him out for a walk. I left him sunning for a few minutes then went to bring him in. He decided he wanted to stay out and lie in a different spot, so I left him having a visit with Katie and Rastus. I peered out at him every couple of minutes. He still wasn't howling, so I asked Dirk to look out the window at him. There he was at the bottom of the bank in the long grass! The poor fellow must have been feeling really mobile today and decided to take a walk on his own! The way down was well padded with long grass, so he was unhurt. But I felt terrible that I could let him fall twice and within a half-hour! He seemed quite happy as we lugged him back up the hill and into the house. Maybe the fresh air will make him sleep tonight! Earlier he was out for his walks with me and also lay in the grass with the puppy playing by him. So, you see, I'm not such a good caregiver to him. Well, I'm off to bed early tonight.

Love, Joanne

Walk in Beauty

As I walk, as I walk,
The universe is walking with me.
In beauty it walks before me.
In beauty it walks behind me.
In beauty it walks below me.
In beauty it walks above me.
Beauty is on every side.
As I walk, I walk with Beauty.

Walk in Beauty is an old Dine prayer, a gift from the People, author unknown, submitted to the Newf-List by
  Ries van Schelvan
  IRELAND

Hi Claire,   **Henry was 17yrs 5mo 24days**
Things have been busy today after an exhausting night with Henry. Today I had to strip down stalls and reorganize. Velcro has gone to her home. Male puppy has figured out how to escape from his run so I had to move him to the barn where it is safer.

We are going to be away tomorrow and managed to get the neighbors to critter sit. I think they actually enjoy it! I don't like to ask them too often, though. They are wonderful and patient with Henry. Weekends are family days with us. Even though the boys are sixteen and fourteen now, we usually spend weekends together.

Gotta run, Joanne

Hi Claire,   **Henry was 17 yrs 6 mo 12 days**

Henry has been keeping me up all night. He seems to like going for several walks. He is getting to be barely mobile, now. But, he seems to be wanting to be waited on starting right about 2:00 PM to about 3:00 AM. Then he wants breakfast, etc again at 6:30 AM. So, I'm not getting much sleep. I don't know how to tell if he is in pain. He seems to feel okay most of the time. He is so thirsty all of the time, he keeps calling for more drinks of water. If I leave it by him, he dumps it. He won't go to it so I have to keep bringing it to him.

Right now, he just had his breakfast and knows I'm at the computer. Already he is whining. Then, he starts the heavy breathing. Any second he will put on his really pathetic whine. If he really has to go, then he will howl.

Well, he is putting on his sad whine and heavy breathing combined. I had better go and see what he wants. Have a great day!

Joanne

Title unknown – Author unknown

A faithful dog will play with you and laugh with you or cry.
He'll gladly starve to stay with you nor ever reason why.
And when you are feeling out of sorts,
Somehow he'll understand.
He'll watch you with his shining eyes and try to lick your hand.
His blind, implicit faith in you is matched by his great love,
The kind that all of us should have in the master up above.
When everything is said and done I guess it isn't odd,
For when you spell dog backwards,
You will get the name of God.

Submitted to the Newf-List by
    Ruth Landmann
    California   USA

Hi Claire,   **Henry was 17yrs 6mo 15days**
    Henry seems to be feeling pretty good. I got up only once
with him last night at 2:00 A.M. (Weekends are family days.) We
went out this morning and he slept in. I arranged for him to be
looked after but wanted to get him fed and walked first. He was
in a deep sleep and we couldn't wake him. He seemed really
comfortable, so I arranged for him to be fed at noon. It was
unusual but seemed to do him good. Ken and the boys don't
like the name I have called the puppy. I really liked to call him
Seymore. But they hate it! So, we have to compromise. It will
likely be Nash or Bubba.
    Well, goodnight. I'll get to chapter three in the morning.
                    Take care. Joanne

Hi Claire,   **Henry was 17yrs 6mo 22days**

Early this morning, Katie was barking like crazy. I threw on some clothes and went out to see what was wrong. I figured on checking on Tarea while out there anyway. But, Katie took me straight to her stall. There was Tarea with her newborn foal behind her, still in the sack, but sitting up. I think Tarea knew that I would come right away. Katie is really a terrific help! Anyway, the colt is doing fine and I got to bed at 5:00 A.M. for a couple of hours. I fed the horses early and Henry actually slept in! Great guy!

                    Joanne

—— HENRY FOREVER: The Gift of Life——

Joanne Seabloom

Joanne is being called.
Old Henry her faithful friend,
Always whimpers, keeps her up past ten.
Never enough time to rest,
Newborns in distress,
Every day starts the same.

Sometimes she thinks she is going insane.
Evenings, Henry takes his walk.
Arabians start to do their talk.
Buddy asks for his grain.
Luckily, there is no rain.
Out to the doghouse she goes,
Opens the door and sees a nose.
"Mommy, Mommy," the baby cries, "she's got some food."
    What a nice surprise!

With permission of the twelve year old author,
    Jessica Arnold
    British Columbia CANADA

To the Newf-List,(midnight) Henry was 17 yrs 6 mo 22 days
Hi There,

    Since I have had a few requests for a Henry update, I thought
I'd send a post to the list.

    For those of you new to the list, Henry is the oldest living
Newfoundland (that anyone is aware of). He was born Dec 6,
1980.

Henry has always been an active dog, but these days are spent with the old fellow lounging around. His legs are a bit weaker due to lack of exercise. For entertainment, Henry listens to his favorite Country Western music station every day. Of course, despite the fact that we prefer rock and roll, we listen to country also. I think his best entertainment at the moment is our 9 week old puppy, Nash. Since Nash started to play in the yard around him, I notice that Henry likes to stay outside longer periods of time. I worried that the little fellow would be too rambunctious and be trampling Henry. But, he seems to understand that he has to be careful around Henry. If he gets a little rough too close to him, then Katie steps in and corrects him. It is really interesting to watch. It is really cute to see Nash carefully step up to Henry and give him a lick on his mouth. Rastus, on the other hand is such a big fellow and loves to cuddle. I constantly have to watch that he doesn't sit on Henry, if I am sitting with him. They all like lots of attention and I think Rastus feels that Henry is getting the most. So, of course, I try to spend extra time with him as well!

Henry's old pal, Buddy Boy, likes to visit and graze around him. He feels his way around with his whiskers. In case you didn't know, he is a 38" tall Shetland pony.

Anyway, Henry is still happy and feels good most of the time. Many times, I have thought the time was nearing to say goodbye. But then, the old dear surprises me and is perky again.

We wish you and all of your Newf family a happy and long life!

Joanne, Henry, Katie, Rastus, Nash

Henry was 17yrs 6mo 23days

Dearest Joanne, Henry and gang!

Wow, am I glad to see how well Henry is doing. He is included in my 'special' thoughts every day . . .what an old dear he is. I know how limited time is when one has a senior guy to take care of. . .it always delights my heart to see and hear anything about Henry. . . he is one very, very, special guy . . .and hearing and seeing things about his remarkable adventures really had helped me to ease into accepting that my old one has gone on. . . it also gives me heart to know that these wonderful dogs seem to be living longer than many of us had originally thought. . . so very, very nice to see an update on this wonderful guy . . . and all your other wonderful friends. . . give Henry and all the gang a big hug and kiss from us here.

Donna Quinta, Osa and Sammie, always loved and never forgotten

Virginia   USA

To Joanne,   **Henry was 17yrs 6mo 24days**

"Rescue one . . . Until there are none."

I vote for Henry for president. Obviously intelligent, wise, affectionate, loyal and dignified.

Sylvia Jones
Nevada   USA

Hi Claire,   **Henry was 17yrs 7mo 6days**

Henry has taken a bit of a turn for the worse. He started to really slow down and barely walks. He kept diving toward the basement stairs and I thought that it was because he got mixed up, being blind. So I kept him away. Despite making gates, etc., he seems to gravitate towards the stairs. After he got hung up on the gates, I padded the basement floor so that he wouldn't be hurt from a tumble.

Well, the cats, Sally and Teetoo have been quite noisy and alerting me anytime Henry wanted something. Last week, Henry tumbled down the stairs. I felt just awful about it! I was sure he was hurt as he had probably fallen a half hour before I got there.

Ken lifted him back onto the big horse blanket, as he had moved off. Henry just lay there. I sat with him and dribbled water in his mouth. He is always thirsty. I sat with him all night and massaged him. I thought his time was up. Then, I realized he was stretching and smiling. He was enjoying the attention. I helped him up and he walked a few steps so I was able to help him onto his clean quilt. It appeared nothing was wrong with him. I read him his story and finally went to bed for an hour. Well, it seems that Henry and the cats have been trying to tell me for a long time that he wants to be in the basement! I can't lug him upstairs to go out. He has no desire to exercise. He likes to have his bedding changed immediately after he relieves himself. Usually I can be right there for him. But I have to be realistic, I can't look after him this way forever. I am the only one in the family who looks after him usually. So, I thought you should know how things are looking with the old dear at the moment.

Last night I was up between Henry and Tiki. She is due to foal anytime but her legs have stocked up terribly. She looks like she could have toxemia. These things of course happen always on a weekend when the vet is busy. But I think there is not much he could do anyway. So, of course, she is wanting tummy rubs and leg rubs too! Tiki is a five year old Blue List, Al Khamsa Arabian mare. Well, I have to go and clean stalls. Ken is home and wants to take me out for brunch, so I'd better get cracking! Have a great day!

Joanne

Good-Bye Henry

17yrs 7mo 15days

Henry 1st
December 6, 1980 – July 21, 1998

Never was there a more loved Newfoundland.
Henry will live in our hearts forever.

Joanne, Ken, Dirk, Brock
Katie, Rastus, Nash, Maxzi

PART THREE

PART FOUR

RAINBOW BRIDGE

Just this side of Heaven is a place called Rainbow Bridge. When an animal dies that has been especially close to someone here, that pet goes to Rainbow Bridge. There are meadows and hills for all of our special friends so they can run and play together. There is plenty of food, water and sunshine and our friends are warm and comfortable.

All the animals who had been ill and old are restored to health and vigor, those who were hurt or maimed are made whole and strong again, just as we remember them in our dreams of days and times gone by. The animals are happy and content, except for one small thing; they each miss someone very special, someone who was left behind.

They all run and play together, but the day comes when one suddenly stops and looks into the distance. His bright eyes are intent; his eager body begins to quiver. Suddenly, he breaks from the group, flying over the green grass, faster and faster. You have been spotted, and when you and your special friend finally meet, you cling together in joyous reunion, never to be parted again. The happy kisses rain upon your face, your hands again caress the beloved head, and you look once more into those trusting eyes so long gone from your life, but never absent from your heart. Then you cross the Rainbow Bridge together.

Author Unknown

Submitted by Walt Parsons

TRIBUTES

GOODBYE HENRY — FROM AROUND THE WORLD

❤ ❤ ❤ ❤ ❤ ❤ ❤ ❤ ❤ ❤ ❤ ❤ ❤ ❤ ❤

Thank you to Henry's Friends   July 28, 1998

Dear List Members,

    I want to thank you for all for your kind messages & cards & poems. It helped ease the pain of losing my beloved Henry. You are truly a great bunch of friends. I was planning to answer the many messages personally but find that I just can't do it. Please know that I really appreciate your kind words, but I can just manage to write this note to the whole list.

    Henry went peacefully. He remains in my heart.

Thank you.

Joanne

Katie, Rastus, Nash

❤ ❤ ❤ ❤ ❤ ❤ ❤ ❤ ❤ ❤ ❤ ❤ ❤ ❤ ❤

Dear Claire,

It was very hard for me to say goodbye to Henry. Once I made the decision, I had to deal with it. I had to let the list know of course. But then about 800 messages arrived. Everyone was so kind. But it made it very difficult for me to use the computer. I cried my heart out every time I tried to read the letters. I couldn't bring myself to delete them. But, things are getting back to normal now. The boys started back to school today. Dirk into grade 11, Brock into grade 9.

We got our Landseer puppy, Lucy. After losing Henry, I was a bit hesitant to get her after all. But as it had been arranged, we went ahead. I wish she could have met Henry. She is a bundle of fun & we are very glad to have her. She and Nash are best buddies. Nash is 20 weeks old.

Well, got to run. I have to make supper.

Joanne, Katie, Rastus, Nash, Lucy

From Joanne to the Newf-List

Yes, I had wanted the vet to come out when it was time to have Henry put to sleep. But he was busy & they asked me to bring him there. This was before they had an actual clinic and worked out of a shed at their house. Kirk, our neighbour drove my minivan while I sat next to Henry on the back seat. Kirk lifted him out and we sat under a tree on the front lawn where Henry's head was in my arms. He went peacefully. ❤

Joanne and Family,

You are right! Never was there a Newfoundland so loved by so many. He was lucky to have you all for a family. You will have thousands of great memories I'm sure, so be thankful for all those many years. We had never met Henry but, by all your posts, pictures and descriptions of him, he was a tremendous guy. We hope the passing was peaceful. He deserved that.

Bill and Ingrid Ball

Murphy, Bailey, and Kelsey, still with us in spirit

Ontario CANADA

A Poem For Henry And All Newfs

If you heard a mournful sound,
From Newfies sleeping in the night,
And you don't know what they are thinking,
But you know something's not right.

Tonight the Newfie howl was long and low.
Another Newfie had to go.

At night the Newfies howl for great dogs gone.
They howl for loved ones at the bridge.
Sometimes at night the howl goes on and on.
You know they hear it at the bridge.

Tonight the Newfie howl was long and low.
Another Newfie had to go.

Sometimes they have to howl to guide the way,
For one who cannot quite let go.
Other times it is to show respect,
When great Newfies have to go.

Tonight the Newfie howl was long and low.
Another Newfie had to go.

Though you think that they are sleeping,
When you hear that mournful wail,
Then you know that they are speaking
To Newfies on the trail.

Tonight the Newfie howl was long and low.
Another Newfie had to go.

This time the howl was heard round the world,
As all around the world the word was spread.
The oldest one among us had to leave,
And every Newfie bowed it's head.

Tonight the Newfie howl was long and low.
Another Newfie had to go. ❤

With permission of the author,
  Marjorie G. Gilbert
  North Carolina USA

I would love to prepare a "Rainbow Bridge Memorial" for Henry if you wish.
Walt Parsons
California USA

Dear Joanne, Ken, Dirk, Brock, Katie, Rastus, Nash, Maxzi,
I will pray for Henry that he may have a good journey home. With love and respect,
Ries van Schelven
IRELAND

Dear Claire,
Do you remember the postcard site with a Henry card? "Bear? What Bear?" Well, it's one of her top fifteen cards out of eighty! Not bad for a Great Dane site!. Also, Ginnie has added Henry's card picture to her Dogware T-shirt line! She has mailed me one which was awfully nice of her. It should be here any day now.
Joanne
(Ginnie Saunders)
South Carolina, USA
Here is the post card site:
< http://www.ginnie.com/virtualcard/DaDaneMail.html >

Hi Ginnie,

Thank you, thank you, thank you !!!!! I just got my Henry shirt! I just love it! Thanks so much! I will really treasure it. I have to say, I shed a few tears, but happy ones. I tried it on right away and it fits too! I really enjoy your site! Thanks again,

Joanne

There will never be words to console you in this loss. All I can say is that my thoughts and my heart are with you. A copy of Henry's virtual postcard is sitting on my computer desk. A good friend sent it to me two weeks ago when we helped them through the loss of their beloved Newf. Henry will live on in many, many people's hearts.

Bonnie Urban
Wisconsin USA

We are deeply saddened by the passing of your beautiful Henry. I know he has touched the hearts of everyone on this list and he will be greatly missed. You and your family should take comfort in knowing what a full and happy life you provided for Henry with all the love you shared. Our thoughts are with you.

Cathy and John King, and Thor
New Jersey USA

To All at Seabloom,

We are sorry to hear of Henry's passing. Never having met him, just seen him on his web page, he was the Newf-L Mascot to us. Long will he be in our memories and our hearts.

Allana Kew and Michelle Rickmond
California USA

Joanne,

This is one of those rare moments when words absolutely fail me. There is simply no way for me to express, to the fullest, my sympathies. While we on the Newf-L will all miss the Henry stories and are burdened by a heavy heart, our sorrow is no-where near your grief. I truly believe that we all thought Henry would simply live forever - that our companions were mortal but that Henry had been sprinkled with some kind of pixie dust. Now, I suspect, Henry has been touched by an angel and will no doubt get His wings quickly. I can just see him flying around the heavens. May the hole in your heart heal quickly with loving memories of Henry and all the joy he brought. God Bless,

Pamela van Giessen, Zillah, Allegra and Company
Illinois USA

We have only been in Newfs and on the list for a year but felt that we knew Henry for all of our lifetime. Your stories brought us great joy and insight to Newfies. Our deepest sympathy and condolences.

Lenny and Beckie Podleckis
New Jersey USA

Marjorie Gilbert wrote:
Hi, (Joanne)

Ever since I sent you my other poem after Henry died, I wanted to write one that was Nash telling Lucy all about Henry. This is the result, such as it is. Sammy did his Newfie Howl again last night and it reminded me I'd never sent this one to you.

Nash And Lucy

Is it true what they say about Henry?
Lucy said to Nash one day,
Is it true that you knew Henry?
Did he live as long as they say?

Yes, it's true what they say about Henry,
Nash boasted to Lucy that day.
Yes it's true what they say about Henry;
Seventeen years, seven months, fifteen days.

I really wanted to meet him.
People spoke of him with such awe.
I really wanted to meet him,
To touch him with my very own paw.

I'll teach you the things that he taught me.
He made me promise not to forget.
He told me of all the things he'd seen,
Wisdom I'll never forget.

I hope I can remember
All the things he said to me.
I just hope that I can always
Remember all that he taught me.

There's a whole wide world out there,
Good and bad and in-between.
Henry said this is a good place,
And he would know with all he'd seen.

He taught me to make a map in my head,
So I never will lose my way.
He told me this is a good family,
Right here is where I should stay.

He said there are three things that we must do,
All three, not just one or two,
To pay him back for all he's taught,
For all that he said is true.

Stay when you find your family.
This one is ours right here.
Make them give you attention,
And scratches behind the ears.

But the thing that only we can do,
The thing we must never forget,
Is to look at them with deep brown eyes,
Make them know Henry loves them yet. ❤

(With permission of the author, Marjorie Gilbert)

Joanne,

I know this will be only one of hundreds of messages you will receive, but I had to let you know how shocked and sorry I am to see your mail tonight. I know they can't go on forever, but Henry was the one who seemed to defy that rule.

I've read every post of yours about him with ever growing admiration for his and your spirits. He was a giant among a giant breed and the unending care and attention you gave him was an example to us all.

Although words can never express enough at times like this, I would like you to know that I feel like I've lost one of my own dogs because you were so kind to let us share his life with you.

I know when I tell Mary in the morning that she will feel the same as I do. She has taken great delight in telling people that I know someone from the Internet with a dog who was seventeen years on the 6th of December.

There are so many things I wish I could say to help, but I'm almost totally useless at times like this, specially through tears. I hope you find comfort in knowing that you have done as much as possible to make his life as great as possible and that I'm sure he appreciated everything you did for him.

Yours in deep sadness, Martin

Martin and Mary Magorrian,

Merlin, Lercio, Hagar and Echo

Braintree, Essex ENGLAND

Joanne and family,

I'm so sorry to hear of Henry's passing. Through you, he touched so many lives . . .It's hard for me to find the right words at a time like this . . .Thanks for sharing him with us. I will miss him.

Annie Divelbiss
Ohio USA

Love beyond boundaries . . .
Sorrow beyond words . . .

From all of us in the Watt family, Carol and Elvis
New Jersey USA

Hi Claire,   (an after thought)

I guess I thought he would live forever. That's why I liked the name you chose for our book. Have a good day!

Joanne

I truly don't know what I want to say to all of you. There's never an easy way or a right time to lose a loved one, two or four legged. But you gave Henry such a wonderful time for longer than many Newfs even are on our earth. It's obvious, from the way you wrote about him, how much you all loved him, and how much he loved you. I know how it feels, because I've been there too many times, too.

Please get the book Dog Heaven, by Cynthia Rylant. It's a children's book that adults also find comforting.

You all have my sympathy.

Sincerely,

Lynne Rutenberg

New Jersey USA

Dear Joanne & Henry's entire family,

We know that words are useless at a time like this. Please know that there are several hundred, if not thousands, of people caring along with you all tonight. Thank you for all the pictures & stories of Henry. You and he were an inspiration to many.

Sleep tight sweet Henry and rest in peace. We loved you too.

Barbara and David Brown

California USA

Joanne and Family,

If only they could live as long as your beloved Henry. My thoughts are with you and your family in hopes that your sad hearts will mend soon.

Joan Steik,

Washington USA

Hi there from Cape Town, South Africa!

I am so impressed with your Henry. I can but wish that I have the same good fortune!

If you don't mind my asking, what did you feed him? Was he a fussy eater? I have six Newfs and love them all dearly. Thank goodness they aren't fussy - they will eat the fridge too, I'm sure, given half a chance!

Regards,
Janeen Hattingh
Charmante Newfoundlands
Cape Town, SOUTH AFRICA

Joanne,

I'm so sorry. I am sending you a poetry collection. I know it will be hard right now, but these are some wonderful tributes to our wonderful friends.

Ruth Landmann
California USA

I am saddened by the news. My deepest condolences to you and your family.

I have Henry's postcard as a background on my desktop. It was this afternoon that I explained to one of my colleagues who this Newf is and what he represents to us Newfy people. I will surely miss reading about him. Sincerely,

Magida Phillips
Pennsylvania USA

I never knew you. I never met Henry. We rarely spoke via the list of exchanged mail. Right now you probably have 500 letters of sympathy. This is one more. But it also is a letter of thanks for showing us that maybe just maybe, our Emma will be a part of our lives for as long as you were gifted. Thank you, and God bless Henry.

Don Robinson
California USA

My deepest condolences . . .I have not been on the list for long but one thing has always stood out and that was everyone's love for Henry. I loved to read the stories. I marveled at his life and the wonderful family that he was blessed with. I am thankful to have known him. I wish I had met him. My life is richer, thank you for sharing Henry with us.

Pat Johnson
Northern Ontario, CANADA

Joanne,

I was saddened to hear of Henry's passing. My thoughts and prayers are with your family today. I think you should write a book about Henry's life. What a great story that would make. I send you Newfie hugs and kisses.

Chuck (Charlotte Holtzen), Calypso & Hootie
Illinois USA
(spending the summer in Marquette, MI USA)

Hi,

My deepest sympathy for Henry and you guys! What happened? Was it just old age and he went to sleep? I hope you didn't have to make the decision for him. We just put down our fourteen year old last week. She told me in her eyes that it was time. She looked so tired. I hated to put her down but she let me know it was time. Again, my deepest sympathy.

Kathy McFadden

Michigan   USA

Kathy McFadden's Newf, Velvet, at age fourteen, won the Oldest Living Newfoundland Award in 1995. See NEWF TIDE Second Quarter 1996, Page One.

Hi All,

We want to extend our deepest regards on the loss of Henry. It is always a very sad time when one loses a loved member of ones family. He will be waiting for you at the Rainbow Bridge and just think of how young and full of life he will be when you are reunited. Our 'Arry' will be waiting with him and we look forward to that day. Can you imagine all the Newfs and their owners together again. What a wonderful thing to look forward to. God bless you at this time and our thoughts are with you.

Douglas and Christel Hill, Ortona Newfoundlands

Alberta, CANADA

To the whole Seabloom family and four dogs,

I am very sorry for your loss. I have said goodbye to many dogs over the years and it never gets any easier. They all die too young. My oldest is not ten and every day I am thankful she is still with me. I hope your Henry will meet my Thor, Lex, Jessie and all my gang. I am sure they are having a great time waiting for us.

Newfly,

Pam Jackson

California USA

Oh Joanne,

How can I be so bereaved about a dog I've never met? Yes, I sit here with tears running down my face as if he was one of my own. I guess Henry was ours just as I feel you are family in some mysterious way. Henry will live in my heart as well. It was your love that kept him here. Go in peace, dear Henry, we'll all look after your Mom. Much love and sorrow,

Jane Richter, Sara, Ben, Pudge, Minnow and Stevie

Massachusetts USA

To Claire

Yes you have my permission, of course to mention my name. Please remind me of the web site address so that I can read about Henry again and write Joanne a note.

Miri Abramson - DVM

ISRAEL

Dear Joanne,

I'm so choked up I don't now what else to say, except I'm sorry. Like everyone else on the list, we will miss the stories of Henry's life and how he was doing. I hope he crossed over in his sleep as peacefully as he lived his life with you. He will always be in our hearts and on our minds. Thank you for all the wonderful stories you let us be a part of. Love and prayers from us all here at Gorlins Newfs.

Lin Watkins
California USA

Our sympathies are with you. It was a very long time to be able to enjoy Henry.

Sue and John Miller
Tennessee USA

Dear Family of Henry,

Your stories have been an inspiration to all of those of us who love Newfoundlands. He touched a lot of lives. We really appreciate your sharing Henry with us. Our thoughts are with you. We will hug our Newfs in Henry's memory.

Ted and Melanie Peck
New Hampshire USA

I'm Free

Don't grieve for me, for now I'm free.
I'm following the path God has laid you see.
I took his hand when I heard him call.
I turned my back and left it all.
I could not stay another day,
To laugh, to love, to work or play.
Tasks left undone must stay that way.
I found that peace at the close of the day.
If my parting has left a void,
Then fill it with remembered joys.
A friendship shared, a laugh, a kiss,
Oh yes, these things I too will miss.
Be not burdened with times of sorrow.
I wish you the sunshine of tomorrow.
My life's been full, I savored much;
Good friends, good times, a loved one's touch
Perhaps my time seemed all too brief.
Don't lengthen it now with undue grief.
Lift up your hearts and peace to thee.
God wanted me now. He set me free.

(Author unknown)
Submitted by Landmann

Goodbye, Henry, indeed! He and his owner have been an inspiration to all of us. What courage and good cheer both have shown!

Kim Stanley
Kansas USA

Dear Joanne and Family,

We are so sorry for Henry's death. I am sure that everybody will miss him, because he was a very special Newfy. Please accept our condolences and be sure that we will pray for him. With our deepest sympathy,

Your friends
SPAIN

Just read the Henry story and it's easy to admire the love in your family. Henry was certainly lucky to find you too. Thanks for sharing.

Louise and Pete Jandacek
New Mexico USA - (praying for moisture desperately)

Dear Joanne and Family,

There are no words I can think of, just know that Henry will always have a special place in many, many hearts around the world. We have felt honored to share in his life through your posts. Thank you for letting us all into your lives and allowing us to know such a special guy.

Patti McDowell and the gang
Pennsylvania USA

I feel I have lost a good friend. I am sure you must feel more so. He beat the odds for a long time and maybe was ready to join all of our Friends at the Rainbow Bridge. My sincere condolences.

Pat Young and crew
Maryland USA

Joanne and family,

I am so sorry for your loss. Henry was such a part of this group and I am sure that we are all missing his loss as well. Please take heart that he is now resting at the Rainbow Bridge. Thank you for sharing Henry with us and letting us enjoy Henry's love for life. Love,

Cyndi Min and Yoyo
California USA

Hi All, (to the Newf-L)

My deepest good wishes.
I need only read the re: on today's post and knew of the passing of "Dear Henry." I glanced to my left and placed a little kiss on Henry's picture which hangs right next to my computer. Before I met the wonderful people in Newfdog and became a member of the list Henry was already my ambassador into Newfdom.

Please take solace in all the love this one "Gentle Giant" has acquired during his later years from all over the globe.

With a special place for Henry in my heart, I remain Newfondly yours,

Camille Mercurio
New York USA

My heart is with you on your loss of Henry. What an ambassador to the breed he was!
Glenda Jones
Oregon USA

We are ever so saddened by the passing of Henry to the Rainbow Bridge. Rest assured he is reveling in his new-found ability to not only see, but to bound about like the puppy he thought he still was.

I'm pretty sure he also got the Newfie equivalent of a standing ovation when he entered that fine place, for he must surely be legend there as he is here.

He will be remembered by many for a long, long time. He was also, I might add, placed on Earth with the best people he could have been. He was a lucky boy that led a wonderfully happy long life with you. Remember him well, and look forward to those kisses you will one day receive again. The kisses of a puppy with a heart full of gratitude. Until that time carry him in your heart and remember that he waits for you under the cool oak tree at the base of the Rainbow Bridge.

Good luck on your new journey Henry. We all love you.
GAD (Gary Donahue)
New Jersey USA

Sleep in peace old friend. You were special.
Jane Kulesa
Colorado USA

144

I never met Henry, but I'm sitting here with tears streaming out of my eyes knowing that I will now never have that opportunity. I have so enjoyed getting to know him through your Newf-L posts. He was blessed to have your love as he blessed you with his.

Nic Rosenau and Rhon Blake
Minnesota USA

(Sharing their home with Moonshadow's WB Kotter - a very gentle Newfie, Gabby - demon possessed rescue cat and possibly Singapura mix, Sadi - dignified, refined, classic rescue cat, Ureialpha, 4 legged and Norwegian Forest Cat mix, Marmalade the shy but friendly cinnamon rescue gerbil and Creamsicle the very silly golden rescue gerbil)

Dear Joanne and Family,

Our deepest condolences to you on Henry's passing. He was truly the greatest Newfoundland ever. The love he generated in total strangers who never met him is beyond words. Heaven is blessed to have Henry. We will miss him. Love,

Vicki Abtin, Queenie and Reba
Utah USA

Good morning Joanne,

Dad and I want you to know our love and thoughts are especially with you this morning. Xoxoxo xoxoxo Henry will be sorely missed by all of us and always remembered with love and devotion. Forever your own loving Dad and Mum.
xoxoxoxoxoxox   X Here X Here ❤
(Gordon and Geraldine Welburn)
British Columbia   CANADA

I don't know what to say except I know how much Henry will be missed. I feel like I knew him through the wonderful stories about him. I'm glad he lived a long and wonderful life.
Lori Linder, Bear and Hensley
Missouri USA

Lend Me a Pup

I will lend to you for awhile, a pup, God said,
For you to love him while he lives,
And mourn for him when he's dead.
Maybe for twelve or fourteen years,
Or maybe two or three,
But will you, till I call him back,
Take care of him for me?

He'll bring his charms to gladden you,
And should his stay be brief,
You'll always have his memories
As solace for your grief.
I cannot promise he will stay,
Since all from earth return,

146

But there are lessons taught below,
I want this pup to learn.

I've looked the whole world over,
In search of teachers true.
And from the folk that crowd life's land,
I have chosen you.
Now will you give him all your love,
Nor think the labour vain,
Nor hate me when I come to take my pup back again?

I fancied that I heard him say,
"Dear Lord They Will be Done."
For all the joys this pup will bring,
The risk of grief we'll run.
We'll shelter him with tenderness,
We'll love him while we may,
And for the happiness we've known forever grateful stay.

But should you call him back,
Much sooner than we've planned,
We'll brave the bitter grief that comes,
And try to understand.
If, by our love, we've managed,
Your wishes to achieve,
In memory of him we loved,
To help us while we grieve,
When our faithful bundle departs this world of strife,
We'll have yet another pup and love him all his life.

Author Unknown

147

My condolences regarding Henry. Even though I never met him, I felt I knew him because of the posts. He truly was loved by all of us, near and far.
Gail White
Florida USA

Hi Joanne and Claire,
Yes, you may use our name. In the time we have known about Henry, we have lived in Denmark and Canada.
Lars and Marij Erup and the girls
Quebec, CANADA

Unbelievable Grief. I want to tell you how much all of us care about Henry's passing. We were all graced with Newf joy due to his touch upon our lives. The memories of Henry's life you so generously shared with us will remain a tribute to him and serve as a model for all Newfoundlands. His life's stories were a continual celebration. I am fortunate to have known him through you. Henry I salute you, mourn you, miss you and loved you.
Sylvia Jones
Nevada USA

Joanne,

I wish some dogs could live forever with us not only in our hearts but in the flesh. There are a few Newfies that I wish I could have met or will meet personally and Henry was the top one. As my old ones creep up in age I hope I can do for them what you did for Henry. We here at KaraBleu are saddened by the loss of Henry. Our thoughts and prayers are with you.

Rick and Donna Humphreys
California USA

Dear Joanne and Family,

Words cannot express how much I hurt for you right now. I know only too well what you are going through. I don't know if I told you but I lost Alvin as well. I didn't post it to the list because I was just in too much pain to actually see it in print. Know that my thoughts and prayers are with you. Fortunately for us their memories lie on in our hearts forever so they're never fully gone. Hugs and tears,

Vicki Limparis
Arizona USA

Dear Joanne,

I am so, so sorry to hear you have lost Henry. I hope it was a peaceful leaving. He had a special place in all of our hearts. I know you loved and cared for him so well. His memory will bring you peace.

Beverly Eichel
North Carolina USA

149

Oh Joanne,

My whole heart and soul is with you. I feel pain too. Henry was a very special dog to me because he made Piper and me feel so much better during her illness. I will never forget that. Your Henry stories made so many people happy He was a King of Newfs and now he is with Piper as he said he would be and surrounded by all the other News who have crossed over. He will be forever watching over you. I am so, so sorry for your great loss. All my love and more,

Carol Batchelder and crew

New Hampshire USA

A request to the Newf-List from Denmark

I have redesigned my homepage and I would love to bring the beautiful story of Henry, the Newf who was our mascot and was more than seventeen. Of course, with all the credits to Henry's Mom. I can't find the story on my hard disc and I can't find an e-mail address for her. I can't remember her name, only something with "seabloom."

Can somebody on the list help me please? And please excuse if I have missed something about Henry's Mom I should know. Thanks a lot in advance.

Kirsten Bjorneboe, Bastian and Einstein, the Newfs

DENMARK

Groetjes   (Note - as it appeared on e-mail)
Kirsten
     Hallo het adres is
http://www.geocites.com/heartland/prairie/1649/henry.html
     Peter Zuyderwijk
     HOLLAND

Hi Peter,
     Thank you for the URL (address) to Henry's story.
     Groetjes,
     Kirsten
     (DENMARK)

Joanne,
     I thank you and all those around you that made our Henry's life so wonderful and happy. I knew that he would not be with us much longer. We are all so very sad because of his passing, but I know he will be so happy and have the adoration of all those Newfs that are waiting for him at the Bridge. Henry has been the most loved Newfoundland in the world, and I feel privileged to have known him. We will miss him, and he will be remembered in my heart always.
     Jean Hain
     Iowa   USA

Joanne and Family,

I'm so sorry to hear about Henry. His life was a celebration and because of the wonders of the Newfie List so many came to know about him. How all of you found each other was meant to be. Give your Newfies a hug and may your many memories help to ease the emptiness.

Ann Thibault
Michigan   USA

Dear Joanne and Family,

The tears are flowing in Portugal in memory of our hero, Henry, and for your sad loss. This was the day I hoped would never come. Henry was unique and his tales brightened this list. Although many of us were not privileged to meet him, I'm sure I speak for everyone when I say that we truly came to know and love him through your posts. The love you shared was so obvious and will continue to be an inspiration for us all. The world will forever be a sadder place without him. However, I'm certain that his noble presence at Rainbow Bridge will be a comfort for all those who arrived before and those, sadly, who will join him in the future. Heaven has a new and very special angel. Henry could not have had a better life or family to share it with. You must have so many special memories that I'm sure Henry will live forever in your hearts, as he will in the hearts of people all over the world.

Goodbye Henry, be at peace, run free and wild and watch over your family who loved and cared for you so much and who are hurting and grieving so badly right now.

Much love to you, Joanne, and to your family and the animals who must also be suffering from his loss. Our thoughts are with you.

Judi Miller, Ziggy, Bear and Oscar
PORTUGAL

Dear Joanne, Ken, Dirk, Brock, Katie, Rastus, Nash, Maxzi,

It is with a sad heart that we say goodbye to Henry but we are secure in the belief that you will be reunited at the bridge. May this poem by Isla Paschal Richardson be of some comfort to you.

> Grieve not,
> Nor speak of me with tears,
> But laugh and talk of me as if I were beside you . . .
> I loved you so -
> T'was Heaven here with you.

Al and Naomi Gofberg
New Jersey USA

Dearest Joanne and Family,

I am so sorry and my heart goes out to all of you and all of us today. Henry's courage and grace will long be remembered. He was all that these wonderful dogs stand for. We will all miss this gallant guy. HE WAS THE BEST OF THE BEST. Love,

Donna Quinta, Osa and family, and of course, Sammie, who is happily greeting and playing with beloved Henry today.

Virginia USA

A Poem From Donna Quinta

> Alone I walked
> Filled with pain
> Deepest despair
> Then lifted my head
> And saw the stars
> And found you there.
> Go in peace dearest Henry

I've lost a Newf - I share your pain. My deepest sympathy.
    Elaina Kintgen
    Indiana   USA

Dear Joanne, and Family,

I was very saddened to read your post this morning about dear Henry. I feel like I've lost a friend. But, I am also happy when I think of what a wonderful life you gave him. I am sure you will miss him greatly as will his companions, Katie, Rastus and Buddy Boy. I hope Buddy Boy is o.k. I know they were special friends. Henry is a great inspiration to all of us who wish our Newfs to live long, happy lives. I'll bet this very minute he is running and sniffing, and seeing and playing and swimming - and sniffing enthusiastic "thanks" to you who gave him the very best care and love, and to us who cheered him on through his time on earth. Run free Henry!
    Judy Van Dyke
    Maryland   USA

The Power of the Dog
By Rudyard Kipling

There is sorrow enough in the natural way,
For men and women to fill our day.
And when we are certain of sorrow in store,
Why do we always arrange for more?
Brothers and Sisters, I bid you beware,
Of giving your heart to a dog to tear.

Buy a pup and your money will buy,
Love unflinching that cannot lie,
Perfect passion and worship fed,
By a kick in the ribs or a pat on the head.
Nevertheless, it is hardly fair,
To risk you heart for a dog to tear.

When the fourteen years which Nature permits,
Are closing in, asthma, tumors or fits,
And the vet's unspoken prescription runs,
To lethal chambers or loaded guns,
Then you will find, it's your own affair.
But, you've given your heart for a dog to tear.

When the body that lived at your single will,
With its whimper of welcome, is stilled (how still!)
When the spirit that answered you every mood,
Is gone, wherever it goes, for good,
You will discover how much you care,
And will give your heart for the dog to tear.

We've sorrow enough in the natural way,
When it comes to burying Christian clay.
Our loves are not given, but only lent,
At compound interest of cent per cent.
Though it's not always the case, I believe,
That the longer we've kept 'em,
The more do we grieve.
For, when debts are payable right or wrong,
A short time loan is as bad as a long.
So, why in heaven (before we are there),
Should we give our hearts to a dog to tear?

Submitted by Ruth Landmann

Dear Joanne and the rest of Henry's family,

I started crying today at work when I read of Henry's passing and I have continued to feel the loss of this great dog. I know you all must be devastated, for although we can anticipate the end, it is always more difficult than we sometimes think it will be. I have taken much joy from your tales of Henry, even in his declining years when he had such a hard time. But what a wonderful family he was chosen by! I know that your love and careful attention made his life one of joy and happy anticipation.

I know that Henry is at peace now and enjoying playing with the other Newfs at the Rainbow Bridge. I truly believe that we will see our pals again, for how could dogs of such great spirit

156

and heart not have souls that would endure? I hope I get to meet Henry someday when the time comes and I see my own Newfs. I'm sure that Henry is enjoying lots of Newfy licks and kisses from the other kids!

Our thoughts and condolences are with you and we will say a special Newfy prayer tonight for Henry and for his loving family. With Newfy love,

Jamie Jennings in Dallas with Jolly, Nate and Meg
Texas   USA

(In response to a request from Claire)

We would be honoured to be included. Joanne loves her dogs and we proudly honour that. And Henry - well he is already a legend.

Cheryl and Roger Acford
Sydstan Great Danes
AUSTRALIA

The Cru extends it's heart felt condolences.

Judi and Pat Randall (The people)
Lucy, Lori, Chuckie, Clara, Anjelica, Maryjane, Lola and Maddy (the Newfs) Gennie (the Komondor) and Dinah (the cat)
Texas   USA

My condolences, Henry was a beautiful dog and was much loved.

> You'll see my face in the clouds,
> Hear the wind whisper my name,
> Always remember me,
> As I remember you.

Elisabeth Heath
Montana   USA

Hi Joanne,

Having visited your web site and read Henry's story, he was a truly lucky Newf to have found such a loving and understanding home to settle into. This really is the sort of new start in life that all of those in rescue would dearly love for every Newf that is rehomed.

Whilst I did not follow the stories on the list, my wife, Deborah visited your web site some time ago and read and enjoyed Henry's story there.

Nigel and Deborah Barlow
Darktarn Newfoundlands
IRELAND

Dear Joanne and Family,

My family send their condolences.

He truly was a gentleman who saw the lighter, brighter side of his life despite his age, and an inspiration to many including myself. This inspiration will live on forever and so honour his memory.

Our hopes that the pain of your loss will soon be replaced by his warm memories.

From Friends on the Newf-List

What a wonderful tribute to a wonderful dog!
Our condolences to you all.

Ellen Toll Katz and the "girls"
Massachusetts USA

Dear Joanne,

Not only will he live in your heart forever, he will live in the hearts of so many people on this list. We are sorry for your loss. We felt like we knew him so well through all of your wonderful posts. We'll light a candle for Henry tonight. Regards,

Merrie and Dick Shumer
Texas USA

Dear Joanne and family.

I am so, so sorry to hear about Henry. It felt like I knew him from reading all your stories. It's amazing how our animals bring us together from all over the world. There is a new angel at the bridge now; a very special one.

Newfs are special and rescues even more so. We have a rescue boy here also. They seem to know that you have saved them, that they have a new chance. They give back so much love and ask so little in return but to be loved. I'm sure Henry felt the love you and your family had for him. His life started all over when he became a member of your family and learned to know what it felt like to be safe and loved, fed and warm.

Now he is your special angel, watching over you all, till you meet again.

Take care of yourself and your family and remember all the wonderful times you shared with Henry.

You are in our thoughts and prayers.

Lori Levy
Chelsea and Chance's Mom
Illinois USA

Dear Joanne and your family.

I am sorry that you have lost Henry. He has had a long and noble time with you, and he will not be forgotten by those who knew him. I am including a poem that was written about sixty years ago by a lady from St. John's (Newfoundland) who lost her beloved Newfy boy. The dog came from the Honorable Harold McPherson. It says everything so much better than I ever could.

With a long distance hug,

Jacky Petrie
Newfoundland   CANADA

160

A Little Prayer for Larry

Is there a country, Lord, where thou does keep,
A place reserved for dogs that fall asleep,
Large, airy kennels, yards for hiding bones,
A little river chattering over stones,
And wide, green fields for those that never knew,
A smoky town, an old worn rug or two,
Before a fire where sparks do not fly out?

I like to think there is, and so I pray,
For one young Newfoundland that died today.
He was so full of fun, not very wise,
The puppy-look still lingered in his eyes;
But he was very dear, he'd come to me,
And rest his soft, black chin upon my knee.

Thou knowest him. One night not long ago,
He tramped with me across the frozen snow;
And there beyond the wood, peaceful and still,
We met Thee walking on the moonlit hill.
Lord, keep him safe, wherever he may be,
And let him always have a thought for me,
That I may hear, when I pass through the dark,
The soothing voice, and the friendly bark.

M.M. Brown

It is a lovely story about Henry. I know what it is like to have to rehouse Newf's. I have three at the moment and also two I have brought up from puppies.

I am putting Joanne's story (about Henry) in the Gentle Touch Magazine —which is the Newfoundland Club of New Zealand's main issue, December 1999. I am the Editor.
Paula Moore
New Zealand

Dear Joanne and family,

I am sorry to hear about your loss. Henry sounded like a wonderful dog. I do know what it feels like to loose a beloved pet. We are going to become first time owners of a Newf puppy on August 9th. I am really excited.
Please accept my condolences!
Barb Wagner
Pennsylvania USA

Joanne,

I must say. . .I've read this story at least a dozen times. Each time I read it, I laugh, I cry and leave with a smile.
Rachel O'Brien (getting teary eyes just thinking of Henry) and Khiori (wishing she had a mentor like Henry)
California USA

Request From Rainbow Bridge
(Author Unknown)

Weep not for me though I am gone,
Into that gentle night.
Grieve if you will but not for long,
Upon my soul's sweet flight.
I am at peace, my soul is at rest.
There is no need for tears.
There is no pain, I suffer not,
The fear now all is gone.
Put now these things out of your thoughts.
In memory I live on.
Remember not my fight for breath,
Remember not the strife.
Please do not dwell upon my death,
But celebrate my life.

❤

Courtesy of Shari Brooks
From a collection submitted to Joanne by Ruth Landmann

To Our Readers,

Thank you for letting us share the story of Henry 1st with all of you. He exemplifies so much of what we have to come to appreciate about our Newfoundlands.

There was a poem written about another much loved and respected Newfoundland that I would like to share with you now. The author, Lord Byron, understood his dog and honoured him with many of the same kudos that I feel are appropriate to Joanne's wonderful Henry.

Claire Carr

Near this Spot
Are deposited the Remains of one
Who possessed Beauty without Vanity,
Strength without Insolence,
Courage without Ferocity,
And all the Virtues of Man without his Vices.
This Praise, which would be unmeaningful Flattery
If inscribed over human Ashes,
Is but a just tribute to the Memory of
Boatswain, a Dog
Who was born in Newfoundland, May 1803
And died at Newstead, November 18, 1808

Goodbye Dear Henry,
You will remain in my heart and the hearts
of others around the world, forever.
With love and fond memories,
Joanne ❤

THE END

WEB SITES FOR NEWFOUNDLAND LOVERS

HENERY'S HOME PAGE:
< http://www.geocities.com/Heartland/Prairie/1649/
henry.html >

INFORMATION PAGES:
Web site for Dr. Dennis Fetko, aka Dr. Dog
 < http://www.drdog.com >
Newf-List Homepage
 < mailto:newf-l@lists.colorado.edu >
Newfoundland Dog Club of Canada
 < http://www.golden.net/~blacknita/ >
Newfoundland Club of America Home Page
 < http://newfdogclub.org / >
Canadian Kennel Club
 < http://www.ckc.ca/ >
American Kennel Club
 < http://www.akc.org/index.html >

OVERSEAS:
England - The South Eastern Working Newfoundlands page at
 < http://members.aol.com/sewnnewfs/index.html >

Denmark — See Kirsten Bjorneboe's Newfs
 < http://www.image.dk/fpenewfies/ >
Read about Henry!
Holland
Home page for NNFC Nederlandse Newfoundlander Club
 < http://www.newfclub.demon.nl >

SHOPPING PAGES:

Newf Items and Gifts
< http://www.petimpressions.com >
Carol Batchelder "Stevie's page"
< http://www.ncia.net/stevie/index.html >
Doggie Diamonds
< http://www.doggiediamonds.com/ddbreed.html >

Fun and Interest Pages

Seabloom's web page
< http://www.freeyellow.com/members6/seabloom/index.html >
Ginnie's vertual postcards — Look up Henry in set # 2.
< http://www.ginnie.com/virtualcard/DaDaneMail.html >
The World of GAD   Frequently Asked Questions
< http://www.gad.net/ >
Newfoundland Flotilla 1997
< http://ourworld.compuserve.com/homepages/nfflotil97/ >